DUCHYLAND

MARK WALTERS

GoNZo SCHuLe

www.gonzo.schule

ISBN 9798864317419

duchy / *noun* / the area of land owned or ruled by a duke

SPIRIT OF OLD CROCKERN

Digbeth, Birmingham: Vape shops and fried chicken takeaways and "UNITS TO LET" ... The city's coach station is here, and I'm boarding the 104 to Exeter. The riding boots I'm wearing provoke baffled stares.

What's *their* motivation? I wonder, these other passengers. Why are *they* going to Devon on this grey, frosty January morning? Are any of *them* going to summon the spirit of Old Crockern? Doubtful. *They* don't look like the sort of people who have a half-baked revolution cooking in their head and a can of mace in their bag. This bloke Dickwart deserves to be maced, but maybe it won't come to that. And if I mace him, might he retaliate by shooting me like one of his bloody pheasants?

I've only been back two days, back from months in Istanbul. I didn't have to come back, and I don't have to be on this coach. It's not my war to fight, really, but after a two-year plague-enforced sabbatical in Laos (more on that later), followed by a summer of carrying buckets of human faeces for Lady Barstow of Huddleton (more on that later), then that stint in Istanbul, I feel I have to do something genuinely productive — or, at least, that's a passable excuse for why I'm not doing something genuinely productive. I thus said: "I'm writing a book ... Yeah, another book that no one asked for or needs ... This one, well, I'll sort of stand up for the rights of plebs to access the countryside we're currently barred from ... No, not on myself. Me and some randoms from the internet. They have a Twitter account, so I reckon they're pretty much legit."

Coasting along the Riviera Line on the 10.25 from Exeter St Davids ... The train skirts the Exe Estuary, then runs right by the South Devon shore through seaside towns Dawlish and Teignmouth; it turns inland, and there are spires and cottages, farmhouses with chimneys smoking, frosted fields and naked trees and iced ponds ... Protestors board at each stop, more and more as we get closer to Ivybridge. I know they're protestors because they're dressed for a cold, muddy march, not afternoon shopping in Plymouth. Floyd, a middle-aged bloke with a comb-over, tells me he was meant to be in Teignmouth today, sat at a pink table getting people to sign up for Extinction Rebellion: "It's The Big One on April 21st — 100,000 of us are going to parliament!"

"You'll glue yourselves to parliament, like human wallpaper?"

"No, we're not doing the glueing thing any more. It pissed off a lot of the public. People ended up hating us more than the politicians."

"How come you're here today instead, heading to Dartmoor?"

"When I read in the news about Dickwart, I was

fuming. That tosser needs to know he can't get away with crap like that. And, to be honest, last week at the pink table wasn't that successful."

"How many people signed up?"

"Two."

"Three, though, if you include yourself," I say, trying to cheer him up.

"No, I was one of the two."

I sit beside Bristolian brothers Danny and Will on the protest shuttle bus from Ivybridge to Cornwood. Danny, the older brother — about twenty-one — wears a green woollen trench coat; Will looks like a teenage McCartney. Both have guitars, which they played on the train ...

"... The day was just ending, and I was descending,
Down Grinesbrook, just by Upper Tor,
When a voice cried, 'Hey you,' in the way keepers do,
He'd the worst face that ever I saw,
The things that he said were unpleasant,
In the teeth of his fury, I said,
'Sooner than part from the mountains,
I think I would rather be dead,' ...
... He called me a louse and said, 'Think of the grouse,'
Well, I thought, but I still couldn't see,
Why all Kinder Scout, and the moors roundabout,
Couldn't take both the poor grouse and me,
He said, 'All this land is my master's,'
At that, I stood shaking my head,
No man has the right to own mountains,
Any more than the deep ocean bed ..."

Danny points out the window: "Cops, man ... and there

too — more! It'll get tasty later. There's gonna be hundreds of us."

I say, "It's a good turnout, a lot more than I thought would come, but look at the other people on this bus: they look like accountants and florists. I can't see them being up for a ruck."

"The cops will rile 'em up, the bastards, that's what they do. You remember the Kill The Bill protest? No? March 2021 in Bristol. It was about some new law they were trying to pass to give the police more control over protests, which basically meant that you wouldn't be able to protest anything. I was there for that rioting in Bristol, and I saw some people get battered, really done over by the cops. And, to be fair, we gave as good as we got."

Cornwood has a pub, a post office, a village hall; and a stone-cross war memorial, which is the centre of the rally. The vibe is smiles not smashing stuff up, and I don't think anyone's getting maced today. Danny is still keen on a riot, but a man can't riot on himself; that's simply a breakdown. Even if me and his brother chip in, it's just not enough. The crowd is a mass of wellies and beards and knitted jumpers and children and placards — "No Man's Land!", "~~Permission~~ Right To Roam!", "THE STARS ARE FOR EVERYONE". Foil-packed sandwiches nibbled and yummy mummies snacking on bananas and pears. That woman wears a Harry Potter scarf, that bloke a Pikachu hat; a few berets around, a sprinkling of green hair. One man *wears* a blue tent. TV cameras and photographers capture the scene. Over a thousand people — and more people keep on coming.

I grab a take-out Jail Ale from the Cornwood Inn and find a wall to lean on. Under bright winter sunshine, I smoke Turkish cigarettes and chat with Julie, who, when she's not protesting, is a librarian. "Decades I've been coming here," she says, "January through to December, and now, as of last week, it's illegal?! But it's not just about Dartmoor; it's about the whole of England. Wild camping is allowed almost everywhere in Scotland, as it is in Sweden and Norway. Why not here?"

An elderly, beardy bloke in a fedora steps up onto the war memorial to narrate the story of Old Crockern — the moor's ghostly guardian, who rides out at night on a skeleton horse. "The tale is that, once upon a time, a rich merchant came to Dartmoor, bought up lots of land, and blocked the public from it. The local people were furious, and one of them summoned Old Crockern, who appeared before the merchant and swore to 'Tear out his pocket!' The merchant ignored Old Crockern, which was a mistake. Over the next years, the merchant was cursed in his efforts to monetise the moorland and, at last, went home poor!"

The crowd: "WOOOOOOO!!!"

"Does that merchant remind you of anyone?!"

The crowd: "DICKWART!!!"

And here I'll explain a little about that div ...

Dickwart is Dartmoor's sixth-largest landowner. He's a millionaire hedge fund manager, not a farmer. He bought his Dartmoor estate — 4,000 acres; that's 2,200 football pitches — in 2013, and when he bought the estate, he knew that people had been wild camping on Dartmoor for generations. He then used his millions to challenge that right in the High Court — not just the right to camp on land he owns, but to camp anywhere on Dartmoor. Last week, he won that case.

A poet is next up on the war memorial, and up after him is Supreme Leader Shrubsole — more scientist than anarchist. He talks about the injustice of the High Court ruling, says that Dartmoor was the last 0.2% of England where legally people could wild camp, and says there should be more places where it's permitted, not none at all. He says, at the moment, we're channelled like ants on footpaths across the countryside, missing out on many of its wonders, and that we need a Right to Roam Act that will defend and extend the public's access to nature. He ends with: "Let's go to Stall Moor to summon Old Crockern!"

The crowd: "WOOOOOOO!!!"

The march along the lane to Stall Moor — part of Dickwart's estate — is a mile-long python fronted by drummers and tambouriners. A chant is boomed: "... F-R-E-E camping must be wild and free on Dartmoor! On Dartmoor! ..." The fella next to me carries a placard that says, "I don't even like camping, but I think you're a dick!" Others declare: "Write To Rome!", "Born To Be Wild (Camping)!" Someone says, "We need to be back for 18:00 so we can lock up our chickens, else the foxes will have them." Another person recounts their crusades in the anti-nuclear protests of the eighties. Homeopathy is a popular topic, as is global warming. When we walk past the entrance to Dickwart's drive, where a few private security mountains are standing guard, *boooooooooos* ring out. When we walk past a white bedsheet painted with "Quiet Please — Horses", everyone whispers. The lane opens onto windy, rugged moorland that's sodden and spotted with rabbit turds. But for a few wild ponies grazing, there's nothing up here: no cows, no crops, no homes.

We form a cloud of sparky defiance on Dickwart's precious moor. Then, just before sunset, with the moorland golden-hued, a druid stands on a rock with a staff in one hand; to his mouth he raises a megaphone: "This beautiful thing that is happening here now — 3,000 people — will in its quiet way be part of history ... Now, Old Crockern: He's today blessed us with fine sun — a good omen — and maybe, just maybe, he'll be willing to manifest in front of us ... Let's call him and see if he comes ... Old Crockern!"

The crowd: "OLD CROCKERN!!! OLD CROCKERN!!! OLD CROCKERN!!!"

Then, over the brow of the moor, comes a greyish, greeny equine beast and a merry pagan troupe of elvish women, jiving, skipping, clapping; shrilling and hollering: "... Wooooooo yah! ... Hey-a-hey-ahhhh ... Yeeeeah! ... Ye-ee-ee-oooooo ..." Flutes, violins, accordions; a medievally, jaunty tune.

The crowd: "WOOOOOOOO!!!"

A little silly, I know, this dingbat dressed up as a myth-ical creature, but there *is* an undeniable energy here. It's not the spirit of Old Crockern that Dickwart should be worried about; it's the very real 3,000-person horde on his land, hell-bent on a cause — zealous enough to be up on a boggy moor in shivery January to deliver a giant fuck-you to one man.

LADY BARSTOW'S FAECES

I've never met Dickwart, but I've carried buckets of human faeces for people like him. That's not a metaphor: I mean literal buckets, I mean literal human faeces ...

After that two-year plague-enforced sabbatical in Laos — which I'll come to — I was broke. My bank balance was negative, and I couldn't borrow more. I had to get a *real* job — one where I'd have to work 40 hours a week, and I'd have to do what a boss told me to do — and that very much pained me because I'd successfully avoided having one for a long, long time. My options were limited because of my schizophrenic resume, and, on top of that, anyone who Googled me would think I'm a degenerate dropout. I couldn't deny that because they would come to that conclusion based on books that *I'd* written that depict me engaged in degenerate behaviour. I had to work for someone illiterate or a criminal or a Christian — the real-deal church-going-type, the sort that believes in second chances and thinks they can save souls. Lady Barstow of Huddleton is one of those Christians — her solution for the Russian invasion of Ukraine was that if we all prayed, really, really prayed for it, Putin would have a revelation and discover Jesus. If Putin could be saved, so could I, which is how I ended up employed at Huddleton Estate.

Carrying buckets of human faeces was only one aspect of the job, albeit quite a large one. The job title was campsite manager; however, though I was the manager, I was also the only one working on that campsite, and I was thus the campsite skivvy too. I managed the bookings and website, and I ran ads on Google. I dealt with the guests during their stay and cleaned the facilities. I was also security, booting out naughty campers: Three times I was close to a brawl; I was once so close that I ran off to swap my flip-flops for riding boots so I'd be better able to kick, and I returned not on foot but on my tractor, threatening to bull-doze their tent if they didn't leave there and then. That tractor I used a lot — despite not having a licence to drive it (or even a licence for a car). It was a red, sixty-year-old tractor, and the brakes hardly worked, and the handbrake not at all. I once smashed it into a tree while freewheeling backwards down a hill. The campsite was off-grid and "eco". There was water but no electricity, and the toilets were compostable. To anyone not looking closely, the six toilets looked normal: they were in a cubicle, they had a seat; you wiped your arse with paper and threw the paper into the loo. But what went into the loo went into a bucket beneath the toilet seat, and those buckets had to be emptied and cleaned by someone, and that someone was the campsite manager. Those buckets would have to be emptied a few times a day, so I would be running back and forth, carrying these buckets of stinking shite to a big crate out of smell and sight of the main field.

I soon started causing trouble. First, I said no to the uniform they wanted me to wear: an estate-branded brown apron. Then I refused to attend the estate's monthly meetings, which all the other employees attended, because Monday was a day off for me, and I didn't want to waste an hour of freedom listening to chatter about ragwort and cattle feed. Then ...

"A 20% pay rise?!" Lady Barstow of Huddleton exclaimed. "But you've only been here five weeks."

"Yes, but I'm excelling in every way, and five-star reviews are rolling in. Yet I'm being paid the same as a checkout chump in Tesco. It's a disgrace."

"But the Hop Cabin ... You get to stay in the Hop Cabin for free."

"The *Hop Cabin*: A rather fancy name for a caravan. It's mouldy. The solar power isn't sufficient for the fridge to run, so I'm eating Weetabix with peanut butter for breakfast. I have to wash my clothes in the shower, and every time I have a shower, inexplicably, the bedroom carpet gets wet."

"Hmm ... We can offer you 10% more."

"10% more than the minimum wage I'm on now — the lowest a person in the country can be paid? No, that's still abysmal. 20%, or I'll walk."

A few days later, she folded: "Ok: 20%."

I also, at a later date, threatened Lord Barstow of Huddleton with the Fixed-Term Employees (Prevention of Less Favourable Treatment) Regulations 2002. I won that battle, at last making some use of my law degree from a top-114-ranked university.

I backchatted, and Lord and Lady Barstow of Huddleton weren't used to that, and certainly not from a Brummie nobody. They aren't friends with royalty, but they've dined with them, and if they need the police, they don't ring 999 but phone the Chief Constable — or Jeremy, as they call him — directly on his mobile. Yes, these are connected people; in the class structure of this conservative country, they're comfy near the top, as they have been since birth, and they expect respect everywhere from everyone because of who they are. Of course, the other employees of Huddleton Estate — of which there were a dozen or so — didn't rock the boat. They had too much to lose: their jobs but also their homes, which were included in their employment package. They were neo-serfs, really; most would be there for life. One guy had worked there for sixty years; another had the job that used to belong to his father. Me, though, what did I care? I'd be gone at the end of summer anyway, as that's when the campsite closed for the year.

The campsite was a teeny-weeny crumb of Huddleton Estate. It took up just one of their many, many, many fields. When, in their office, I first saw a map of their land, I could scarcely believe it: "So this and this and this, and that and that, oh, and that too ... That's just half of it?! ... This lake as well? That woodland, yeah? All the way up to there? I see, even further than that ..." The estate was 2,000 acres; as a point of reference, Glastonbury Festival is on a 900-acre spot. Some land was used for crops, and some for cows — about a hundred pasture-fed cows that were so costly to care for that a four-pack of burgers ended up priced at over £8. They did a little forestry, and they had a wedding venue, and, from time to time, a TV show or a movie would be filmed on the estate. A lot of the land, though, wasn't used a lot of the time.

Camping was restricted to the campsite; possibly some people did wild camp elsewhere on the estate, but if they did, I never heard about it, and it would have been easy enough to get away with due to the grounds being so large and it being no-one's job to look for such wicked criminals. If someone had wanted to wild camp instead of choosing the campsite, I'd have understood, even though, as far as campsites go, it was a pretty good one. You see, the thing with a campsite is that it's to wild camping what swimming in a leisure centre is to a swim in the sea. It's nature manicured. You're in a cut-grass field with no real sense of the wild. There are other people there, pitched metres away from you. Even if they're good people, you might just have had enough of every single goddamn bastard on the planet and need the solitude that the wilderness provides. Then there's the cost of camping: £15 for adults, £10 for kids, at the one I managed; so a father taking his daughter out for two nights would spend £50 instead of nothing if they went wild. And there's the point that there might not be a campsite wherever you want to go, and even if there's a campsite in the general area, you have to plan your whole excursion around going there — taking a route you maybe don't want to take, having to work your schedule to be in and out on time.

This isn't a hit piece — I must make that clear. It isn't retribution from a wronged employee. I completed the contract at Huddleton Estate, and we left on okay terms. Though, I admit, if I were available this summer — which I'm not because I'm busy being an insolent jackass on the estates of people like them — I'm not sure they'd have me back. She'd say to the Lord: "He did do quite fantastic work, he absolutely, really did, and he did double the booking numbers and quintuple five-star Google reviews, but, well ... I just don't know, dear ... He was a little nutty, wasn't he? One time, he was on the tractor, and he only narrowly avoided mowing me down; he said it was an accident, and he blamed it on the brakes being faulty, but just

before I leapt out of the way, he had this look in his eye —
a look of pure evil." But a year or three from now, if they're
desperate, and I'm starving and homeless, the chances of
me being back there aren't — unless they read this book —
zero. There are much worse places to work, and feasting on
nature made that job just about bearable, allowed me to
cope with lugging around buckets of faeces. The trees and
quiet and fresh air, daily seeing squirrels, rabbits, birds,
deer ... It was food for the soul. Had I been carrying those
buckets to and fro in a warehouse in Birmingham, I'd have
quit on the first day.

There are much worse people to work for too. They're
alright people, really: There are permissive footpaths
through some of their estate, and some of their woodland
is available for the public. They plant trees. (Though
possibly they receive government subsidies for this; they
receive subsidies for all sorts of things.) They hold positions at charitable associations, and, once a year, they host
a free event where the Lord's choir sings and children are
ridden around on tractors (not the brakeless deathtrap
tractor and only by people with licences). A family of
Ukrainians reside in their attic — which is much less bleak
than it sounds, as the attic has eight rooms and a snooker
table. They gave me a free pack of sausages sometimes.
(Which made me feel a bit like a dog, but, hey, who doesn't
love free sausages?) And I'd occasionally be invited to the
"Big House" (as the serfs referred to it), where I'd dine with
the Lord and Lady, and we'd chat and drink wine, and it
was all very civil and nice — and I'd not rant or swear
when I was sober enough to remember not to.

Yes, they're not, by any real measure, sneering, sadistic
tyrants.

But what they are is disconnected from the masses.

They don't know what it's like to earn minimum wage, to live beside neighbours that have seven kids, to have a garden that couldn't even squeeze in a ping-pong table. They've never holidayed at Centre Parcs, never shopped at Poundland or lunched at Greggs, never spent a sweltering summer in a caravan without a fridge. They don't know what it's like to live in a flat in an urban shithole — or even a detached house in St Albans — and to not have anywhere to escape to where you can be alone in nature for a night, just you and the trees and the stars.

Dickwart, I suspect, is the same. He's likely not sat on a mock throne surveying his estate, taking potshots at passing peasants. After a couple of Jail Ales are in him, he's perhaps an alright bloke. Him and his like just don't know that people need spaces like Dartmoor because him and his like don't hang with that sort of people. Which is why, now and then, it's important for that sort of people to make themselves heard when they're being ignored, for them to arrive unwelcome in a 3,000-person flock and give a bit of feisty backchat. Dickwart definitely heard that.

I don't desire Dickwart and the Barstows stripped of their land and sent to Stoke to carry buckets of human faeces for their lordly sins. This isn't some madcap communist revolution. I lived in a communist country for two years: I know all too well what a shambles that ideology results in. Let people, I believe, hoard a bit of land for their exclusive pleasure: one football pitch, two football pitches, seven football pitches ... Pick a number, and be generous with that number. But hundreds of surplus football pitches hoarded is outrageous.

That excess land must be shared. And if a land hoarder doesn't like any cost or hassle that comes with that, they can sell the land — hoard the money instead.

"TRESPASSERS WILL BE BEHEADED!!!"

Although I managed a campsite for a summer, I never once camped there, but I did wild camp once that summer, and it came about because of a woman I met on the campsite at Huddleton Estate ...

Her name was Siobhan, and she drove a convertible nineties BMW and made shampoo from marshmallow. She said she had some shrooms and asked if I wanted some. I said I did want some. I didn't eat them on the spot because I'd once done a shift at Marks & Spencer on ecstasy, and it didn't go well — gurning at customers, touching children's feet, incorrectly counting change, jabbering nonsense, sweating madly ... (I was on the childrenswear department for that shift, so I wasn't being weird about the feet: I had to measure them for shoes.) After that debacle, I swore to never again do drugs at work, so I pocketed the shrooms and scoffed them for tea.

Siobhan and I stayed in touch, and she later came by on my day off, and we drove to the south coast in the evening. The plan was to camp at a campsite, but we got lost en route — she thought Google Maps makes people stupid, so she didn't want to use it — and the plan thus morphed into camping on a beach. We parked on a side street in West Wittering, a village on the Sussex coastline. After a pint at a pub, we floundered by torchlight along narrow pitch-black lanes to the beach. At the entrance to the beach was one of those signs that said something like, "WARNING!!! CAMPING IS PROHIBITED!!! CAMPERS WILL BE BEHEADED!!!" It might be illegal, I thought, and some pissed-off ranger might have a rant at us, might even phone the police, but, well ... fuck 'em. It was too late by then to find some other place to sleep, and, besides, I *needed* the sea: I hadn't seen it in years — Laos, as well as being communist, is landlocked. So on we went onto the deserted beach. We pitched the tent — dunes behind us, the lapping, black sea in front — and we snuggled together for warmth. We listened to the serene waves, stared into the starlit sky, talked for hours. She fell asleep before me, and, for a while after, I was awake savouring everything: the soft sand, the fresh salty air, the quiet darkness, the purring woman beside me ...

We woke at dawn. The blooming morning was bright and blue, and we could see the Isle of Wight. Siobhan did yoga while I strolled the shoreline, walking a couple of kilometres past pastel beach huts and a little cafe that hadn't yet opened for the day. By 07:00, we'd gone, and there was no trace of us ever having been there.

That night is a glorious memory. Had we obeyed the "WARNING!!!", it wouldn't have happened.

On my walk that morning, I'd noted that the beach appeared to be privately owned ... Hmm, I wondered, how come the beach isn't owned by the local council or the National Trust, as I thought all beaches would be. How did this pretty beach end up owned by West Wittering Estate Limited?

Their own website told me: In 1952, 126 local residents set up West Wittering Estate Limited to buy the beach and the land near it to stop the Church Commissioners selling it off for use as a shitty resort. I thought: Fair enough; no one wants a tasteless holiday joint on their doorstep. And they don't charge for access to the beach; they make money from the car park and cafes. I also thought: Who the hell are the Church Commissioners, and why the heck was it theirs to sell?

The Church Commissioners, Google told me, is an organisation that manages the assets of the Church of England. Its assets are valued at £10 billion — you need to see the zeros to really understand a number like that: £10,000,000,000 — of which at least a quarter is properties and land. It owns about 105,000 acres of land — 60,000 football pitches.

I fell down that rabbit hole for a bit, and I also tried to ascertain if it was actually illegal to camp on that beach: The webpage I skimmed said it wasn't a criminal offence but was a civil one. Before I learned what that meant and the potential consequences, I got distracted — probably by pondering fantasy football transfers — and I forgot about the whole thing until Dartmoor and Dickwart popped up in the news.

Now, as I'll be a professional trespasser for a while, I need to know more about trespassing, and I'd rather acquire that knowledge from someone who's done a lot of trespassing than from WikiHow. Which is why I'm back at Digbeth, boarding a coach — this time to Bristol ...

The "Skill Share Forum" is at Hamilton House, a bland, scruffy building that was once an office for a bank but is now a community centre; on one side of it is a Banksy mural from 1999: a teddy bear throwing a Molotov cocktail at police. In reception is a machine: "Get Tested NOW. This machine offers a FREE sexual health test." There's a table of flyers — one advertises "Magical Creativity Classes"; another, "Buddhafield 2023: Liberation Through Imagination". On the wall is a poster — a couple of kissing snails — for a Psychedelic Society dating event: "Intimate Connection & Juicy Conversations".

I had to book a spot for this — this workshop organised by the same people who organised the protest at Dartmoor a few weeks ago. At first, it was fully booked, and I thought I'd have to trespass the trespass meeting — "I have a right to be here!" — but a few people pulled out yesterday, so I'm here officially, didn't have to barge my way in. "Skill Share Forum" is a mask name for it, and it's what I say to the receptionist at Hamilton House — "I'm here for the, err, Skill Share thingy." Trespass Workshop, the organiser must have thought, isn't the sort of event that even somewhere as liberal as Hamilton House would be keen to host. I don't recognise anyone here, but, from a show of hands, most of the forty people attending today were at the Dartmoor protest. One of the new ones is a hairy fellow: "This is my bible," he says, holding up a well-worn little black book: *The Squatters Handbook*. He says, "All these empty buildings, all these empty bits of land, there's something absurd about it."

Jon is the host. He's a thirty-something, sprightly, slight guy and wears a green corduroy button-up shirt. He says, "We want England to have the same access rights, by and large, that exist in Scotland. In Scotland, there's a default of access; you have a right to be somewhere unless someone can justify why not — and 'It's mine!' isn't a valid reason. In England, it's the other way around: There's a default of exclusion and a few small exemptions for access. In England, we've calculated that, at the moment, we have a right to access just 8% of the countryside and that 1% of people own 50% of the land. We feel that the access rights and land ownership situation right now are totally unjustifiable.

"So, the law, the legal technicalities around trespass ... You'll have seen the signs that say, 'PRIVATE PROPERTY! TRESPASSERS WILL BE PROSECUTED!' Those signs are a legal fiction, effectively. You can't be prosecuted, in a criminal sense, just for trespassing. The act of being on someone else's land is a civil offence in England, not a prosecutable, criminal one. You can't be dragged up in front of a criminal court and sent to jail for a civil offence. In theory, though, a landowner could pursue you in a civil court — the sort of court you'd end up in to, say, settle a dispute with your neighbour about a fence or a tree. But, in practice, no landowner will realistically take you to civil court because it's not worth their time, money, and energy. They'll just tell you to piss off. And then it's up to you if you do that or not. So it's not really the law that's stopping you from going where you want; the obstacle is psychological — it's the fear of that confrontation with a landowner."

Someone asks: "If the landowner is insisting that you leave, and you refuse to, what can they do?"

Jon: "What's typical is that a landowner says, 'Oi! Get off *my* land!' Or they'll shout, 'WHERE DO *YOU* THINK *YOU'RE* GOING?!' They're often angry to start with, and if you refuse to leave there and then, they get even angrier. But if you refuse to leave, there's not a whole load they can do about that. If they attempt physically dragging you off the land, it's them that's committing a criminal offence."

I ask about wild camping; how the law deals with that.

Jon: "Camping overnight doesn't change anything. If you put up a tent, it's the same result: It's a civil offence."

A man asks: "Do you have a minimum acreage that you avoid for trespassing? I know someone who has a five-acre garden; would you trespass on that?"

Jon: "We 100% avoid people's gardens. That's the most common thing we get on Twitter: '*Oooooo* ... You want me to come roaming in *your* garden, do you?!' But we want nothing to do with gardens, and access in Scotland doesn't include people's gardens."

I ask, "How does that work on a huge estate that someone lives on?"

Jon: "On a lot of private estates, you have the house, you have the domestic garden next to it — where there will likely be garden furniture and potted plants and stuff like that — and then you have the huge estate beyond that, that's thousands and thousands of acres, and we'd avoid the house, avoid the domestic garden that's beside the house, but we'll trespass on the big estate."

A woman asks about the police: "If the landowner calls the police, how likely is it that they'll come?"

Jon: "Rural police, there aren't many of them; they're unlikely to turn up for a civil offence. If you haven't threatened anyone or damaged anything, the police shouldn't come. But, still, they might come."

She says, "And if they do come, what then?"

Jon: "If the police come and tell you to get off the land, you might argue the toss, say, 'This is a civil offence. I haven't done anything wrong, blah, blah, blah ...,' but if the police are really set on you leaving, it's probably not worth you persisting; there's a danger that you're straying into a criminal offence at that point, as the police will see it, at least."

She says: "So that means they can illegally pressure you to leave, and, when you resist, they can legally arrest you for not doing what they say?"

Jon: "Yes. As anyone with much protesting experience will tell you, that isn't an uncommon occurrence when dealing with the constabulary, unfortunately."

A man asks, "What could the police arrest you for? What would be the charge?"

Jon: "What you do when you're trespassing, how you're acting on the land, can have potential criminal ramifications ... There's a difference between basic trespassing, which is a civil offence, and what's called aggravated trespassing, which is a criminal offence. Aggravated trespass kicks in if you cause damage, or if you commit violence, if you do anything to disrupt lawful activity that's taking place on that land — like, for example, a pheasant shoot. If you, say, take wire-cutters with you and start cutting up barbed wire, as you might feel inspired to do, that would be criminal damage, would be aggravated trespass. There's also a public disorder offence that trespassers could maybe fall prey to, plus, potentially, what's called breach of the peace; in both cases, it basically comes down to violence or the threat of it."

The man says, "Have you had any problems with the police?"

Jon: "No, no problems, no arrests, no one taken to civil court, and that's partly, I guess, because we strictly stick to a non-violent, non-destructive approach to being on land. Our mass trespasses, we make sure they're sort of nice and fluffy; there are picnics, and we take violinists and ornithologists, and we learn about wildflowers."

I ask, "If the landowner takes you to civil court, what happens then? Do you have to pay them something?"

Jon: "If you disrupt something the landowner is earning money from, that gives the landowner impetus to take you to civil court, and you could potentially end up paying the costs of that disruption. Say, for example, there's a bunch of toffs on a pheasant shoot, and they're paying £3,000 each to kill these dumb, defenceless birds — 'Ah, what a great day out!' — and their day gets cut short because of whatever you've done, you could be left reimbursing the landowner for any lost income resulting from that."

Squatter Man chips in: "It's a legal tort, so the landowner has to prove damage, that you being there has caused them a loss of some sort. The example of the pheasant shoot is true, but it's much more likely that any loss or damage, if they can even prove that you caused it, will be negligible. A friend of mine who was making a crop circle in Wiltshire got prosecuted for trespass. A civil court fined him £7. That was for the damage caused to the specific wheat he'd ruined when flattening it for the crop circle. So the landowner spent thousands and thousands of pounds on this court case, and, when it came down to it, it was all for the sake of £7."

Jon: "And that's why we say, in reality, unless you've done something to really, really piss them off, like, on a personal level, it's very, very unlikely they'll take you to civil court."

DUCHYLAND

Dickwart is only the sixth-largest landowner in Dartmoor, and his 2,200 football pitches there are twice as much as the Barstow's estate. Why go after third-rate gentry or hedge fund wankers when there are bigger cheeses to grill? How about, maybe, the biggest cheese in the country, Charles III ...

The Crown Estate is the fourth-largest landowner in England, but the land of the Crown Estate — valued at several billion — isn't actually Charles's. The Crown Estate is a public body, and its profits stream to the government. Most of the profits, anyway, as £80 million a year — 25% — is docked from Crown Estate revenues for the Sovereign Grant: an annual payment to the monarch to fund His Highness's official duties — cutting ribbons, shaking hands ... that sort of stuff.

Charles, though, does own land, and some of that land comes from being the Duke of Lancaster in addition to being the King. 25,000 football pitches of land, named the Duchy of Lancaster, have passed from monarch to monarch since 1399. It's wholly separate from the Crown

Estate; it's Charles's "private estate" and is worth millions annually, all of which he pockets personally. Some of the land is real estate in London, but most of it is rural — in places like Lancashire and Derbyshire and Yorkshire.

Charles, as the Duke of Lancaster, owns a lot of football pitches worth of land; not that he has the most land of the dukes; far from it ...

The Duke of Cornwall — aka Prince William — owns 75,000 football pitches of land, which includes about a third of Dartmoor. Dickwart is a peasant to a person like him — "He's only the *sixth*-largest landowner in Dartmoor? Then, no, don't invite *him* to tea." The Duchy of Cornwall was forged in 1337 by Edward III as a private estate for his son — the 1st Duke of Cornwall — and the land has been the private estate of the heir to the throne from then til now (when Charles became monarch, it passed to William). The land is spread across twenty counties, and £1 billion is the value of the realm. The profit this year was £24 million. That profit is income for William — £65,000 every day.

Charles, William: These are dukes you've heard of, but what about James Spencer-Churchill, the Duke of Marlborough? Or David Manners, the Duke of Rutland? Or Henry Somerset, the Duke of Beaufort? Some own more land than Charles does: The Duke of Devonshire has 40,000 football pitches; both the Duke of Westminster and the Duke of Northumberland have 70,000.

Topping the list of largest landowners in England are the Ministry of Defence, the Forestry Commission, the National Trust, but add up all the land owned by dukes and barons and marquesses and viscounts and earls, and the sum of it puts them at the head of the list by far. There are 24 non-royal dukes, 34 marquesses, 110 viscounts, 189 earls, and 442 barons. So it's a little mathematical sleight of hand to lump them all as one and claim them the largest landowner en masse, yet they are, together, a recognised, named group: the aristocracy. Some own little or no land, but, in total, they've monopolised millions and millions of acres. They have more than all the "ordinary" homeowners combined, who make do with just 5% of the land.

The aristocracy owns at least a quarter of England. That means the aristocracy, essentially, owns a country within a country: the size of the land they own is the size of Belgium. That's how much land they likely have, but no one knows for sure ... The Land Registry charges £3 a pop to find out who owns each slice of land. At 25 million parcels of land, that's £75 million to reveal the map in full. Well, not quite in full ... 15% of land in England is unregistered. The Land Registry website says much of the land owned by the aristocracy "has not been registered because it has never been sold, which is one of the main triggers for compulsory registration".

The dukes, I know where some of their land is: a website called Who Owns England? has some of their estates mapped clearly out. Some dukes have shown their hand so they can claim subsidies and tax breaks — by giving the public limited access to their land, they can skip taxes on inheritance, for example: "I suppose you can visit *my* gardens, *my* beautiful parkland and estate, if you really must do, but only on this day or that day or that day, and you must be gone by 17:00, and you *must* — I repeat — MUST stay on the path. You'll need a ticket, of course: £25 ... But if you work for the NHS, I'll give you 5% off."

It's the dukes I'll target for several reasons: 1) They're the heads of the aristocrats; in the peerage hierarchy, they outrank the others. 2) They — bar a few — have tens of thousands of acres each. 3) None of it seems to be earned bounty — as could be argued is the case with, say, James Dyson, the bagless vacuum cleaner bloke. He owns more than some of the dukes, but at least he paid cash for his acres in recent memory; at least he added value to the world. Even damn Dickwart bought his Dartmoor estate. But the dukes and barons and whatnots ...

Some dukes, it's their land on the basis of being the ancestor of a bastard kiddie of a long-ago king: The 1st Duke of Richmond — Charles Lennox — was one of seven illegitimate sons of Charles II, and today's Duke of Richmond — Charles Gordon-Lennox — is the 11th one to hold the title and huge estate. Henry FitzRoy, the 1st Duke of Grafton, was also an illegitimate child of Charles II. We're onto the 12th Duke of Grafton now — also called Henry FitzRoy — and Euston Hall and its surfeit of football pitches (6,000) have been passed along from the 1st to the 12th in a direct line.

Other dukes hit the jackpot from Henry VIII's dissolution of the monasteries ... The Act of Supremacy in 1534 made Henry VIII "Supreme Head of the Church of England" and made the Pope a turd. For people who thought the Pope wasn't a turd but was, in fact, God's agent on earth, this change was problematic; and that was a lot of people, as until then, England was a Catholic country. Why would Henry do that? Because he married a Spanish princess, Catherine of Aragon, but later wanted to ditch her for his new fancy, Anne Boleyn. Divorce, though, wasn't permitted by the Catholic Church. The Pope refused an exception for Henry, so Henry told the Pope to sod off, told him that England would abandon Catholicism, told him that he — Henry — would govern the Church of England and that he'd then grant himself a divorce. Henry did that, and as part of his tantrum, he stripped Catholic institutions of swathes of their land. Henry handed that land to his pals. This happened nearly 500 years ago, but that land is still mostly owned by the ancestors of Henry's mates. Take Woburn Abbey, for example: That land — 7,000 football pitches — was taken from its monastic residents and handed to John Russell, the 1st Earl of Bedford. That land is *still* with the Russell family — it belongs to Andrew Russell, the 15th Duke of Bedford.

Then there are the dukes who's great-great grandpas were friends with William the Conquerer ... In 1066, William arrived from Normandy to conquer England. He won the Battle of Hastings in October and was crowned on Christmas Day that same year. His coronation ceremony was the first to be held at Westminster Abbey, beginning a tradition that still persists. Since 1066, it's been the location of the coronations of 39 monarchs — Charles will be the 40th this May. William claimed all the land as his. He then carved it up and handed parcels to his best buds. Twenty years after William's conquest — according to the *Domesday Book* — the 190 barons that were William's best mates had half the country in their pockets. And a dozen of them, William's bestest besties, had half of that half. The 6th Duke of Westminster — Gerald Grosvenor — when asked for advice on how to be successful, quipped, "Have an ancestor who was a very close friend of William the Conqueror."

Go to their land now, go to stroll, to picnic, to lounge, and the dukes will shrug at that soiled history and instead depend on today's law: "This land is *mine* by law, and the law is the law, so get the hell off *my* land!" But the law, well, it's not always right, is it? And who made those laws? And who were they representing? Because before 1832, only one in a dozen men could vote, and no women could vote at all ... Laws change, anyway, if enough people dispute them — or even if enough people ignore them. Laws have, actually, changed previously to the detriment of these dukes: The Parliament Acts of 1911 and 1949 and the House of Lords Act 1999 weakened their powers. The latter of those said, "No one shall be a member of the House of Lords by virtue of a hereditary peerage." Until then, these dukes were automatic members of the House of Lords — one of the two places, along with the House of Commons, where the laws of this land are created and amended. For centuries prior to 1999, the House of Lords had included several hundred members who inherited their seats; not just dukes but a whole bunch of aristocracy. And from 1721 — when the country had its first Prime Minister — to 1900, *the vast majority* of Prime Ministers were aristocracy: William Cavendish (4th Duke of Devonshire), Charles Watson-Wentworth (2nd Marquess of Rockingham), Augustus FitzRoy (3rd Duke of Grafton), William Petty (2nd Earl of Shelburne), Edward Smith-Stanley (14th Earl of Derby), Robert Gascoyne-Cecil (3rd Marquess of Salisbury) ... A diabolical situation indeed: The landed privileged luxuriating in Westminster, smoking cigars, pushing through legislation that benefitted themselves, voting down anything against their interests.

England doesn't need dukes, and the dukes don't need all that land, and we know this because previous dukes have disappeared, and no one misses them. The Dukes of Newcastle became extinct in 1988, and what was their land now belongs to the National Trust. And 1964 saw the end of the Dukes of Leeds — a title first bestowed in 1694 — after neither the 11th nor 12th dukes had a son. The 11th duke had a daughter, and there was a piece on her in a 2015 BBC documentary called *The Last Dukes*: She's called Camilla Osborne, and she's not a duchess, has no estate. She lives in a pleasant, modest house. She transitioned from the aristocratic lifestyle to a relatively simple one and seemed unscathed by the downgrade.

In the same documentary was a segment on the Duke of St Albans, who still has the title but no longer has a stately house and thousands of private acres. The seat of that dukedom was in Nottinghamshire; that house is a hotel now, and the estate is a gigantic council-owned park — "varied landscape and wildlife ... popular with walkers and cyclists". The duke now lives in a terrace house in London. It's a nice joint on an elegant street, and he has a little Thai maid, so no need to worry about him. I'm sure the other dukes look down on him, but it's not like he has to heave around buckets of human faeces to survive; he's doing alright. Though he has suffered: He said in the documentary, "Up to a few years ago, one used to get a quarter of a deer twice a year from Richmond Park, but that was stopped by Tony Blair."

Then there's the Duke of Manchester ... landless too after Kimbolton Castle was sold in 1950 and turned into a private school, and Tandragee Castle was let go in 1955 — it's now the HQ for a crisp company called Tayto. Alexander Charles David Drogo Montagu, the Duke of Manchester today, was born and raised in Australia and later emigrated to America. He's been married three times — to two of them simultaneously for a while — and his first wife claims he tried to shoot her with a speargun in their kitchen. He did a spell in prison in Australia for fraud and was again charged with fraud in the US when, in 2011, he bounced a $3,575 cheque to Speedy Car Loans. Then, in 2017, he was sent to High Desert State Prison in California for five years for burglary — the woman burgled said the Duke of Manchester was shirtless and shoeless in her home in Las Vegas at 02:30; when spotted, he dropped a box and ran off. He's still the Duke of Manchester because dukes can't ever be sacked for literally anything.

The dukes can keep the titles; they can keep the money, even keep the damn house, but the land ... No, they can't keep that, not to hoard for purely their own use. I'll pay some visits ... I won't make appointments, queue up, beg: "Please, Your Grace, please, please ..." I'll just go and get on with it, roam and camp as if the land were the land of the plebs. I'll go first to Lancashire, where is Charles-owned Whitewell, then I'll bounce around the country, visiting dukes: I'll go to Eaton Hall, owned by the Duke of Westminster, and Chatsworth House, where the Duke of Devonshire resides. I'll drop in on the Duke of Bedford at Woburn Abbey, and I'll stop by London to check out what dukes have what there. Then to the realm of the Duke of Richmond and the Duke of Norfolk's kingdom. I'll end with a visit to William's Duchy of Cornwall.

Will this probably be pointless? Probably, yeah, it will.

And for this probably pointless endeavour, will I end up being arrested? Maybe, yeah ... Definitely maybe, as I'm messing with connected people, people who when they call the police — "There's a bloody rascal on my land!" — the police come.

Maybe, on the other hand, it will be fine ... In 2014, I was told *very clearly* — by the Chinese authorities them-selves — not to go to Xinjiang (a "problematic" region in China), and my visa wasn't valid for there; I just went anyway, and it was fine. And when, in 2018, I travelled overland through the Americas — Mexico ... Nicaragua ... Colombia ... — to the Amazon, where I went into the depths of the jungle to drink a shaman's brew, that too was fine. People say things — "Can't go there! ... Too dangerous there! ... You'll be arrested! ... You'll die!" — but, most of the time, that's bullshit; normally, everything's pretty much fine, and I'm 73% sure that visiting Duchyland will be too.

CHARLES III'S BOOZER

I'm sat in Charles III's boozer, loafing in an antique armchair beside a roaring wood fire, a pint of Moorhouse's Blonde Witch in hand, with my shoes and socks off. The decor is reds and brass and well-worn woods; there's a grandfather clock, and on the walls are old portraits — kings and dukes — and sketches of cricket games and fox hunts. Bottles of wine sell for £130, and a woman nearby says to her friend: "My granddaughter Beatrice has bought a horse; here, I've a photo ..."

Definitely royalists here, and no chance of coaxing anyone to my cause: It's on par with rocking up to an Extinction Rebellion parade — "We're doomed! Doomed, I tell thee!" — to say, "I *like* that it's getting warmer." Or striding into St. Paul's Cathedral: "You know Jesus, the Bible, all that jazz, is it really true or is it ... *bullshit*?" No, they won't be on board with that; toe the line or get the hell out. And I won't bother the bar staff or waitresses — "1265! ... John of Gaunt! ... Robbed!" Minimum-wage monkeys — don't know, don't care; they're not paid to deal with that, not paid to answer stabbing questions spouted by muddy Brummies. No, say nothing weird, no rants about Henry IV ... Got to *seem* normal — as normal as possible for a barefoot bloke in a posh pub. They don't trust me as it is: When I order a bowl of chips, the waitress says, "You will, um, pay for this, won't you? You won't ... run off?" I wasn't offended; truth is, I had considered legging it: Free chips! But, no, I'll pay — now I know I'm being watched.

The Queen dined here in 2006, and I bet *she* didn't pay. She came as part of celebrations for her 80th birthday, and I know what she dined on as a folder of newspaper clippings about that day is proudly displayed on a table here: *The Daily Express* ...

> "**A First Pub Lunch For The Queen**: Her visit to the Inn at Whitewell — a 14th-century hostelry in Lancashire — came during a trip to one of her favourite parts of the country ... She dined on cottage pie and apple crumble tart ..."

The Daily Telegraph says what else she got up to that day ...

> "The Queen and the Duke of Edinburgh yesterday visited the estate of the Duchy of Lancaster ... Her Majesty and His Royal Highness visited Radholme Laund Farm, Cow Ark ... Afterwards, they visited Puddleducks Tearoom in Dunsop Bridge ... They also visited Burholme Farm ..."

On the reverse of one of the clippings is another story from that day ...

"The scale of pensioner poverty in Britain is a severe indictment of the failure of our welfare state. We supposedly live in one of the wealthier countries in the world, yet a large swathe of our elderly population have to endure a bleak retirement, struggling on meagre payouts ..."

My bare feet aren't a deviant protest against the King. I had to take off my shoes and socks, no doubt about that; I *had* to — they're so damn soggy and soiled. You see, I walked here from Cow Ark, and in doing so, I look like I've crawled here from Bolton. Cow Ark isn't that far away, six or so km, but I walked here through Duchy fields — or, more precisely, Duchy bog. A taxi from Clitheroe dropped me at Cow Ark, and after ten minutes of walking along a quiet lane, walking past sheep in grassy fields — *baaaaaaaa* — past thorny hedgerows and rocky streams and rusted barbed wire and stinging nettles, I found what I was looking for: on the right, by the side of the lane, quite discreet: a black sign on two wooden posts; on it was a coat of arms, red and shield-shaped with three gold lions; the sign said: "DUCHY OF LANCASTER. WHITEWELL ESTATE".

The Duchy of Lancaster, the Duchy of Cornwall, neither have public maps of their land. They don't want us to know all that they own, and it's not security concerns because Charles and William are almost never on that land. I did email the Duchy of Lancaster to ask for a map, but they blanked me; they didn't even say, "Sorry, we're unable to ..." — just a straight-up snubbing. So I turned Sherlock: I took to Google Maps to see what I could find, and I scouted around the Inn at Whitewell, which I knew was a Duchy premises; Charles owns 6,000-ish acres around that joint, but from where to where did the estate stretch? I found that sign, and I guessed that it probably marked the southern boundary of the estate — a start point.

I kept to the lane for a while, then scaled a stile and took to a footpath that would take me right through Duchy land. A public footpath, so I had a legal right to be there; one foot off that footpath, though, would be trespassing — and I definitely shouldn't be camping. Another stile led to peaty bog, and I regretted wearing Converse and black skinny jeans; they're entirely inappropriate for this sort of endeavour, but I wore them because I didn't want to look like a hiking geek — very uncool, those guys. I was also regretting the weight of my bag; I'd not even gone that far, but already it was pissing me off. I packed sensibly: No mace, no drugs, nothing sharp — no toothbrush shank ... nothing that burns: no fags, no lighter, nothing that makes me a "fire risk" ... No, give them nothing easy to pin on me. 9 kg in total, and I stuck largely to essentials — tent, airbed, sleeping bag, clothes, water, food — but I refuse to be a crustie, so some luxuries did make it in, in case I end up dealing with anyone official: "Sniff me ... Come on, don't be shy ... Bleu de Chanel, Molton Brown — Russian leather ... Lovely, right? And my pants, take my word for it, M&S — Autograph range. And, here, look: my card ... name, number, website ... and note the domain isn't .com or .co.uk; *.schule* — that's *German* ... Why? To indicate I'm sophisticated. The point is: I'm a legit member of society — and you can't prove otherwise without a psychiatrist."

"... Jesus! ... Bollocks! ...," I muttered as I squelched through the mired fields — fields empty and untended; no hope of growing anything in those fields. My feet couldn't have been any wetter, totally sodden they were, and then I sank into a mud pit; my feet were then beyond soaked — a squidgy, horrible disaster. (I could have done with those riding boots. I didn't wear them because they're so tight-fitting that without a doorstep for leverage, they're *impossible* to remove, and there won't be any doorsteps where I'll be sleeping tonight; if I'd worn those boots, I'd have to sleep in those boots.)

I passed through Higher Lees Farm — a Duchy farm; its sign branded with the Duchy shield. It was a grotty dump. I thought with it being a Duchy farm, it might be nice, but no: a rundown farmhouse and knackered machinery, scattered farming detritus — wrecked fencing, broken pallets, holey sacks ... Looked like a scrapheap. As did Radholme Laund Farm — also a Duchy establishment — which the footpath passed through: some static caravans, stacks of manky hay, old tyres; mud and shite everywhere, and warehousey buildings stuffed with cows. A machine on somewhere, so there must have been someone around, but I didn't see anyone. I didn't see anyone the whole way from Cow Ark to the pub.

Half the time, I wasn't on the footpath — at its best, a mildly trampled, muddy line; at its worst, nothing — but I was trespassing *by accident*: I was *trying* to stay on the path but kept finding myself far off it. I needed that footpath as my sense of direction isn't good, and I'd lost phone service, and the OS map that I thought I'd downloaded had, in fact, only downloaded 12%. I say my sense of direction isn't good, but what it may actually be is terrible; yesterday was evidence aplenty for that: I'd booked into a campsite in Clitheroe — about 10 km from here. I got to the campsite, went to the office for the welcome spiel, listened to the directions to reach the field I was on ... but, somewhere, I took a wrong turn.

After a long walk, I called the office: "How far away is this field?"

"A couple of minutes from the office."

"Oh ... Because I'm by Shireburn Kennels."

"Where?"

I was so lost I wasn't even on the campsite any more; I was so far off the campsite that they didn't even know where I was.

Now, though, I've downloaded that OS map at the pub, so I should be fine ...

Out of the pub, I walk past a Ferrari, a Porsche, a couple of Range Rovers, a few Audis ... and turn right past a little church with a graveyard — St Michael's — to take me to some stepping stones: twenty or so to cross the River Hodder. On the other side, stomping again, uphill through bog, through another farm, this one New Laund Farm — a Duchy sign; the red shield, the three gold lions. Tractors and *baaaaaaaa* and that stink of shite again; little stone buildings and milk churns and hay.

Sheep in all the fields here, but these sheep, they don't care that I'm here too, don't care at all. They don't flee, they just stand there looking dopey — *baaaaaaaa*. They're not stressed by someone who isn't a farmer being near them, and none spontaneously combust as I pass by. Even if a few did, well ... survival of the fittest ... I was reading Paul Theroux's *Kingdom By The Sea*, and he was up in Scotland and saw nine sheep drown because they didn't react quickly enough to the tide. They were swimming for a bit — yeah, sheep can swim, and quite well, apparently — but these sheep got caught in the current and gave up in the end. Theroux later met a vet, and the vet said, It happens; sheep drown now and then. So, as I said: Survival of the fittest ... weed out the wussy sheep, clean up the gene pool of the 15 million sheep in England. That's how many sheep there are; *a lot*. A sheep isn't some magical rarity like the Amur leopard or Tapanuli orangutan. It's not a protected species that needs to be babied.

In that book, the same chapter, Theroux was on a bus — in a post van, in fact, as it's so remote up in the far north of Scotland that the post van had to double up as the bus service — and a local, MacGusty, also on board, pointed out the Duke of Westminster's estate up there — 54,000 football pitches — a private reserve where only the wealthy could hunt or fish, and MacGusty said Prince Charles — as he was then — came up on a helicopter sometimes for shooting on the estate. MacGusty said, "It's the old way of life ... It's very unfair." That was in 1982, the year Prince William was born, and nothing's changed: The old way of life still impacts the present; it's still very unfair. And it will still be the case 40, 50, 60 ... 100 ... 500 ... years from now — unless we make it fair.

From that farm onto a paved lane: Some woods to the right here; mossy trees, last year's birds' nests on the naked branches. To the left, empty fields; field after field of empty undulating greenness, daisies and buttercups and wild-flowers, bordered by dry stone walls. A red tractor pulling a trailer of manure drives past, as do flat-capped farmers in Land Rover Defenders. Further on, beside a quad bike, I see an earthy granny in a woolly beanie; she's locking a gate after loading some sheep into a trailer — *baaaaaaaa*. I say, "Is this all Duke of Lancaster land?"

"Aye, nearly all of it is."

"And all the empty land is used for what? For some-times putting sheep on?"

"Aye."

"Nothing is grown here?"

"We don't grow nought round here. Well, a bit of rape-seed, but just a little."

I cross a stone, arched, 18th-century bridge back over the River Hodder, where is Duchy-branded Burholme Farm. More sheep — *baaaaaaa*. I wonder: Do we *need* sheep if they're taking up this much land? Bit of a crappy animal, really, isn't it? If you're four years old, and it's only up against a few others, like a dog and a fish and a bird, you *might* say it's your favourite animal, but a sheep, an insipid, tedious sheep — *baaaaaaaa* — no one of sound faculties has a sheep in their top fifty favourite animals. In Laos, I didn't see a single sheep for two years, and I didn't miss them once.

There's money in them, true — enough money for people to thieve them: In 2021, one man stole £87,000 worth of sheep. The sheeplifter was caught and handed an eight-month prison sentence — which isn't that long and is a risk worth taking for £87,000, especially as the Countryside Alliance claims that less than 1% of sheep thefts result in a conviction. £87,000 worth of sheep is a lot of a sheep, though, and a logistical headache: A sheep sells for £100 on average, so that bloke stole 870-ish sheep. Sheep are large; I don't even know how I'd steal *one* sheep, especially travelling by train. A lamb I could manage, I reckon; a small one would fit in a plastic shopping bag. But how to explain it? On the train, returning to Birmingham, people would ask about it, they would be suspicious about that lamb in the bag — *baaaaaaaa* ... "No, it's not a sheep, actually; it's a lamb ... Yes, it's alive; if that's the problem, I can sort that ... I didn't steal it, no ... I bought it from, err, a man ... No, I don't have the receipt because I paid with, um, Bitcoin."

I walk on, see woods, see ducks, geese, and ... *what is*

that?! A partridge maybe, I've no idea; a brown body with a long tail, a green head with red around its eyes; could be a Peruvian turkey for all I know ... A couple of deer flee once they spot me — they leap full over a fence without pausing, hurdling the thing — and I see a pair of rabbits, big brown ones, running around, playing ... or, actually, I think one might be trying to hump the other one. I recross the River Hodder over an old, iron, green bridge, and I'm in a mucky quagmire. This is bad, very bad, this mud, very awful indeed, and my legit-member-of-society strategy is blown apart: I can say, "Smell me, I smell French, and my boxers are M&S, Autograph range ...," but the fact is if I'm covered in filth, looking like a goddamn medieval peasant, it makes no difference, does it? Some of the filth is sheep shite ... Julie, who I met at the Dartmoor protest, she said human shite is worse than cow or sheep shite, but I don't know ... Mine's not; if *hers* is, maybe she needs to see a doctor. She said out on the moor, she craps on a sheet of newspaper, then folds it up and bags it to dump it later in a bin. She said it's either that or dig a hole with a trowel. I can't be arsed with either of those options, so this morning, I necked a palmful of loperamide hydrochloride (chemical butt plug) — block myself up. A one-way digestive system for a few days ... then, back home, comfy on a toilet, Hiroshitma.

Onto a road now that leads into Dunsop Bridge, and I pass another Duchy sign: Root Hill Estate Yard — barns and stables converted into rentable offices. A signpost says Lancaster is 24 km to the right of here — there's a Duchy office there within Lancaster Castle, which is part of Charles's territory. Clitheroe, the sign says, is 18 km to the left: I spent a day there, a place with Cowman's Famous Sausage Shop and Steve The Cobbler and Banana News —

"Cash Only!" — where people ask "Do you want a brew?" and eat chips with gravy and hot pot pies. I liked it. I took the train there from Birmingham, through Wolverhampton, Stafford, and Stoke, saw pokey, grimed houses, side by side by side, saw patched-up roofs and half-arsed, bodged extensions and rotting sheds; through Stockport and Blackburn, where were council estates and sludgy canals, and runty youths kicking footballs in strangled streets, and people smoking in six-yard junky gardens where greying y-fronts and plus-sized Primark dresses were pegged up on sagging clotheslines.

In comely Dunsop Bridge, a little down the road: Puddleducks Tearoom, which doubles up as the post office; a dozen houses and a stone bridge; daffodils and podgy ducks; a BT phone box — the 100,000th public payphone in the country, it says on the side, to mark the hamlet being the geographic centre of Great Britain. What little there is here is Duchy-owned. It's a cult-type thing, their branding all over — even the kids' park is royalised: Jubilee Play Area. I see a stone cross with wreathes of poppies below — a war memorial commemorating those who gave their lives for England so their ancestors could be barred from 92% of the countryside. I saw another at Clitheroe, in the grounds of the castle there: in a little garden with six feeble flowerbeds was a lone soldier with head bowed in remembrance; the base of the statue listed the names of the dead from Clitheroe — hundreds across both wars. I also saw one outside Manchester Piccadilly; that one in tribute to soldiers blinded in WWI. The plebs penned into 5% of the land, poor bastards conscripted from Manchester and Blackburn, from Clitheroe and Stafford, they were sent out to defend 100% of the land in WWI and WWII, and it will be them again in WWIII.

I head out of Dunsop Bridge along Trough Road and pass a row of cutesy cottages with dark blue doors — Duchy labelled: Jubilee Cottages ... The village hall, then more cottages like the last ones: Lancaster Cottages. The road follows a stream — Langden Brook — and, on the other side of it, the scene is sheepy pastures — *baaaaaaaa* — and scattered trees. Up a slope, this side of the stream, is heathery, purple moor — where, I think, grouse are shot. "The reason they don't want people roaming around that estate," a bloke in the White Lion in Clitheroe told me, "is because they shoot grouse, and that's big business for them, big, big business, thousands of pounds per person per day."

After a couple of kilometres, a sign: "DUCHY OF LANCASTER. WHITEWELL ESTATE". These are the ones they use on the estate's borders; it's the second of those I've seen, the first 10 km from here — as the crow flies. Between there and here, Charles owns it all; all his, and all totally unearned. All his because, in 1265, Henry III seized swathes of England from rebelling feudal lords, and, in 1399, Henry IV declared that bounty the monarch's private property for evermore. That's why today, 600 years later, this land belongs to Charles. All the farms on it, the Inn at Whitewell, Puddleducks Tearoom ... And Charles, via his Duchy of Lancaster swindle, skimming profits off them all to line the pockets of his Gieves & Hawkes £5,000 suits. And this estate is only 15% of his 45,000-acre empire — an empire valued at over £500,000,000.

I turn back the way I came from and head south again toward Whitewell ... Another Duchy sign, where the road runs near the River Hodder: "PRIVATE FISHING". A good patch of grass, a bench ... this will do — I'll have this. There's a waist-high gate across it with a padlock on, but it's not exactly the Berlin Wall, is it? I leap the gate. As dusk settles, my tent is swiftly up.

Surely no one will disturb me: A zipped-up tent out of place somewhere at night — what fool would unzip that tent? Anyone, anything, absolute terror, could be in there: a sabre-rattling Mongolian nudist troll, a decaying, maggoted corpse, Jeremy Clarkson ... Let sleeping dogs lay; don't poke the mutt, no. Walk right by, leave some other sucker to deal with that.

BELGRAVE AVENUE

The Duke of Westminster is, this very moment, at Charles's coronation; he's carrying a royal flag — a VIP role — as he leads Charles's and the Not-Quite-Queen's procession from Buckingham Palace to Westminster Abbey. He's there, and I'm here: outside his manor — which is in Cheshire.

In front of me is an imposing, black gate with golden detailing — pillars on either side of it, stone hounds atop them. A sign yells, "PRIVATE". To the right, on the other side of the gate, is an olde red-brick building — Belgrave Lodge. Far down the drive, an obelisk stands tall, and far behind the obelisk is the Big House.

To the side of the grand gate is a little stone wall — so little that I could step over; I wouldn't even need to climb. And at the far left side of that little stone wall is a little white gate — is it locked? No. I open it, walk in ... I start along the driveway — Belgrave Avenue — an arrow-straight gauntlet bordered by thick woods. I wonder: Has anyone *ever* arrived by bus (the No.1 from Chester to Wrexham, which I got off after twenty minutes) and then *walked* along this drive? No, not likely.

You might think: *That's his drive! You shouldn't go down there!* But I could walk a couple of kilometres along his drive and still not know what cars are parked outside his house. I won't go all the way down to his house — though, even if I did, would that be so wrong? He's allowed to walk down anyone else's driveway, right? If he wished, Hugh Grosvenor — that's his real name, this duke — he could walk down *your* drive and knock on *your* door.

He knows I'm coming: I sent an email last week ...

"I accept my invitation to visit you. I'll arrive on foot and stay in a tiny green tent. I'll wander around a little to see what you're doing with all that land. But fear not, I come in peace, and I won't be a nuisance during my stay. I'm sure you'll know that trespass isn't a criminal offence. Aggravated trespass is, but I won't be doing any aggravating while I'm with you. A civil offence is what trespass is, and you may thus wish to sue me for this heinous misdemeanour. That's okay — you can do that. You can also phone the police; technically, they shouldn't come, what with trespass not being a crime and me being a finely-behaved trespasser, but I understand that if you make the call, they likely will come. That's okay — you can do that."

A guy replied: Dobbs — Head of Family Office & Rural Estates. He said, "We don't condone trespass", but he also said that if I'm coming anyway, let him know when, and he'll tell me somewhere "safe" that I can pitch the tent. Very nice of him — or, at least, so it seemed ... But I didn't email him back because it could also be a trap. The estate is so large that if they don't know when I'm coming or from which direction, it's impossible to keep me out. But if they know when I'm coming and where I'll enter, a crack squad of ex-paratroopers might pounce. That's the sort of thing that this duke can afford. He's worth nearly £10 billion — 11th on *The Sunday Times* Rich List 2023.

Halfway along the drive from the gate, I turn off it into Kennel Wood. I'm on a tyred track, but it's clear people don't come in these woods often: the track is really over-grown; no one could have driven down here for months. It's dense with trees and shrubs; a few soupy ponds. Some dirty-looking mushrooms there, which I won't be foraging, as I'm well stocked with Tesco Luxury Fruit & Nut Mix. Loads of stinging nettles — *ah, ooh, ouch* — and lots of thorns scragging my skinny jeans. I had to bin the Converse from last time — they were ruined. I was down to flip-flops or riding boots or Chelsea boots. I went for Chelsea boots — black, suede. Though unsuitable for the countryside, they're classy. If I meet someone, what will they make of a trespasser who looks like this? These boots, these jeans, these shades ... If I'm better dressed than them, better smelling than them, how will they deal with that? Plus, I got a dictaphone, a snazzy, little Sony. Stick that in their face makes me look like a pro. "Anything *you* say may be used in evidence against *you*." Give them a card — "Yes, that *is* a German domain ..." — and ask *them* what *they're* doing. That will melt their brain; pure Jedi shit.

I roam the woods, a roundabout route, crunching foot-steps, brambles, thorns — *argh, ouch, argh* — and I come out on an opening ... There are grimy plastic containers; diesel in them, I guess. Bits of crap and junk all over the ground: green netting, polystyrene, red-and-white tape, blue rope, a Fudge wrapper, bottle tops ... At the edge of the woods is a field, a field in which they're growing some-thing. Tractor tracks across it; there always is; there's no other way to farm a field. To cross this field, along the margins or following the tractor tracks, and damage nothing is simple. You don't need to be a farmer to know how to cross a field; you can just see it like you can see where and when to cross a road. It just takes a smidge of common sense that anyone older than six has.

I cross that field, then more fields ... Left, over there, the obelisk, and to the right of that, a gothic clocktower — part of Eaton Hall, I think. An orange digger there, paused in motion from Friday. A dog barking far off and the smell of manure, the stuff piled up ... I come to a runway. Hugh could later land his jet here, but I bet he stays in London, spends the night in Mayfair or Belgravia. He owns most of those places. In a *Guardian* article on the most expensive streets in the UK, two of the top five are Grosvenor Square, Mayfair (average house price: £23.5 million) and Grosvenor Crescent, Belgravia (£15.4 million).

Hugh's website says, "The Grosvenor family ancestry can be traced back almost 1,000 years, while its association with London property began over 340 years ago — in 1677 — when land to the west of the City of London came into the family following the marriage of Sir Thomas Grosvenor to Mary Davies." Which is true but is vague on detail. It doesn't mention, for example, that 21-year-old Thomas Grosvenor married Mary Davies when she was 12. That's not a typo: T-W-E-L-V-E. That's how that land in London was acquired.

Hugh's website says, as well, that they trace their ancestry to Gilbert le Grosveneur, who came to England with William the Conqueror. But it seemed from my Sher-locking that Hugh d'Avranches, the 1st Earl of Chester, is the source, and I asked ChatGPT to confirm that, as there were conflicting histories; it said: "The Grosvenor family, including the current Duke of Westminster, can trace their ancestry back to Hugh d'Avranches."

So why wouldn't the Grosvenors say that? Why big up boring Gilbert — thought to be the nephew of Hugh d'Avranches, and who seems historically inconsequential — when they could go large on d'Avranches?

Well, this is the Encyclopedia Britannica entry for Hugh d'Avranches ... "Hugh d'Avranches, the 1st Earl of Chester, also called Hugh The Fat ... Companion of William the Conqueror, who made him Earl of Chester in 1071 ..."

Hugh The Fat in French is Hugh Le Gros ... Interesting, right? *Gros* — *Gros*venor ... Bit of a goddamn coincidence that. Hugh, so the story goes, was so obese he could hardly walk. Yes, not really an ancestor you'd want to publicise.

This land I'm on now is a direct result of that obese French invader. It's in the *Domesday Book*: "Eaton, Cheshire: Owner, 1086: Earl Hugh of Chester." It was seized from someone and given, for free, to Hugh The Fat, then passed on and on and on from then until now, until this Hugh today.

I'm now on a lane through Park Plantation on my way to Duck Wood, walking to the area where I think, based on my scouting of the estate on the OS map, I want to pitch up ... Untamed forest edges the lane, and I inhale the fresh, spring greenness, listen to the soothing birdsong ... I turn onto a muddy track taking me through woodland to Oxleisure Pool; then out the woods and into a meadow: long grass, daisies and dandelions, buttercups and purple wildflowers, butterflies and birds. They're clearly not doing anything with this land here, though maybe animals graze it time to time. In his email, Dobbs mentioned livestock, but I've not seen a single sheep or cow, not even a rabbit or a deer ... Oxleisure Pool is a pretty lake; a few swans in there. Another lovely lake is near it, and the River Dee runs close behind that lake, and over the river is Aldford — a whole village owned by Hugh.

The meadows around these lakes are much, much larger than Grosvenor Park in the middle of Chester, which I went to ... Last night, I stayed in Chester. I stayed at a guesthouse there on a lane called Grosvenor Place, and that lane came off a road called Grosvenor Street, on which is the Grosvenor Museum — and also the Magistrates Court, which I might end up in if charged with aggravated trespass. At the end of Grosvenor Street is Grosvenor Roundabout, and on the other side of Grosvenor Roundabout is Grosvenor Road, where is the Crown Court — to end up there, I'd have to be very, very bloody naughty. Go a little along Grosvenor Road, you cross Grosvenor Bridge ... The other end of Grosvenor Street, en route to Grosvenor Park, is Grosvenor Shopping Centre; and in Grosvenor Park is a Sicilian marble statue of Richard Grosvenor, 2nd Marquess of Westminster, robed and looking like a Roman emperor. The Grosvenors gifted that park to the plebs; they did that in 1867. *Nice!* But the population of Chester has boomed since then: In 1801, Chester had a population of 15,000. In 1901, the population had reached 38,000. It's now 88,000. The park is the same size (20 acres) as it was, but many more people must share it. And, anyway, what's 20 acres out of 11,000 acres, which is the size of this estate? 0.2% is what it is. And this estate is only some of Hugh's rural land. He also has the 23,000-acre Abbeystead Estate in Lancashire, and Reay Forest Estate in Scotland — 96,000 acres — and 37,000 acres near Cordoba in southern Spain, and ...

I drop my bag in the meadow beside Oxleisure Pool, and I lay on my back, relax. The sun is breaking through on what's been an overcast, windy day. I'm surrounded by dandelions, lady's bedstraw, cow parsley; at one with nature in this charming meadow. A yellow butterfly flutters past, and bees buzz from flower to flower. A church — one in Aldford — bongs over the birdsong: *Bong. Bong. Bong.* This is it for today: I'll take it easy right here in this lovely meadow, this meadow that is, after all, really the point of roaming, to discover and savour places like this ... At Huddleton Estate, I got to see off the paths, see what was "PRIVATE", and I saw, and I enjoyed, a glut of joyous spaces like this one right here. Across those 2,000 acres, I could, whenever I wished, skip about naked chasing butterflies. *I* could, but 99.9999999% of people *couldn't*. If they were caught chasing butterflies *au naturel*, there would be a fuss, even though Mother Nature cared not whether it was them doing it or me. While on that estate, I realised that we're being rationed the countryside unnecessarily, realised there was plenty of unused countryside available for people to escape the noise, the hustle, the queues, the sirens, the mad dogs ... An abundance of countryside to escape to that we're for no good reason barred from.

I'll just chill for now, won't put up the tent yet, even though it's unlikely that anyone will come and rant at me: The nearest building, I think, is Black & White Cottages — as the OS map calls them — half a kilometre away, and it's a Saturday today, so aside from the coronation, people on estates just don't work on Saturdays anyway. Farmers need days off, gamekeepers too, and forestry workers, and they just do Monday to Friday because why not? Everyone at Huddleton Estate did that, and I understood that was typical on these sorts of estates. 07:00 til 16:00 was the shift they did year-round there. I'll wait until past 18:00 until I pitch the tent, as if I put it up now and someone does collar me, they'll know where I am and could terrorise me through the night. That's what I'd do if I were them: I'd come back in the night making ghost noises, spraying manure on the tent — teach the cheeky bastard a lesson.

I pick up a little phone signal and watch a video about the loons that have been camping outside Buckingham Palace and along The Mall for days, the poor and the posh alike there for a front-row seat at the royal pantomime. It's like an upbeat refugee camp with Prosecco and PG Tips. A Geordie in a Pound Shop tiara says, "I'm like a five-year-old before Christmas, waiting to open my presents."

Others have taken the opposite stance: there have been arrests of anti-monarchists protesting earlier today. *BBC News* says ...

"Dozens of people have been arrested during the King's coronation ... Accusations of heavy-handed enforcement started early on Saturday when the Chief Executive of anti-monarchist campaign group Republic — Graham Smith — was arrested at a protest in Trafalgar Square. Footage showed protesters in 'Not My King' t-shirts being detained ... 'The reports of people being arrested for peacefully protesting the coronation are incredibly alarming,' said Human Rights Watch UK director Yasmine Ahmed. 'This is something you would expect to see in Moscow, not London.'"

They hadn't really done anything, it seems; they were

simply standing in the street, yelling. I can't be bothered with that. No one listens to people yelling in the street. If I hear someone yelling in the street, my instinct is to take the other side of whatever they're yelling about. As for the Insulate Britain crew glueing themselves to highways ... no, screw them — idiots. The same goes for that business with throwing orange powder on a snooker table at the World Championship in Sheffield, which some Just Stop Oil fool did the other week — in a first-round match, not even the final. That made me want to buy oil — buy it, then pour it down the sink. A protest should be directly linked to the cause you're protesting for. The Animal Rising stunt at the Grand National, fair enough — horses die in the Grand National, so try and stop the Grand National. 118 people arrested there for "criminal damage and public nuisance offences". The result? The race started fourteen minutes late — so fair enough, though pointless. But this, this now ... I wanted to come on this land, and I have done; and I've been here for hours, and I'll sleep here tonight, enjoying myself. If I was just standing outside the front gate, yelling ... waste of time. Hugh's driveway is so damn long that no one would even hear me.

A choir of birds wakes me. I laze a little, dine on nuts for breakfast. A splodge of Molton Brown under my armpits instead of a shower, then I pack up ...

A layer of mist is over the dewy meadow, and I cross it under the morning's golden glow ... I come to a road: I could turn right to reach Aldford Lodge and, from there, leave over Iron Bridge to Aldford — that would be the easy way out. But I'll turn left: walk up to and past the obelisk, and then exit via a back entrance into Eccleston — another village owned by Hugh — where I can walk down Eaton Road into Chester. That route, from here into Eccleston, is about 4 km — right through the centre of the estate.

I walk the road through meadowy pastures, see some geese, a pheasant; I hear a woodpecker, see one of those lodges that I saw at the front gate ... A black railing fence ahead, a gate; I could climb that fence if I need to but let's see if the gate is open: Yes, it's open ... I stay on the road, pass majestic trees; to the right, over long grass and wild-flowers blanketed with wispy mist, is the gothic clocktower ... I come to a crossroads: in the centre is an island of grass, the red-tinged obelisk rising to a tapered point; on one side of it is a blue circle within a stone wreath, and within the circle is a medieval golden gate.

Behind the obelisk is the final stretch of driveway to the Big House; a flag — too far away for me to see the design — flies on a pole from its roof. Hugh's actual garden, his super-manicured private garden — I can see from the OS map — stretches for at least a hundred metres *behind* the Big House. So what's all this *in front* of the Big House? A vast open space, parkland unfurling into the distance. It's not landscaped as Grosvenor Park in Chester is, there are no flowerbeds, but it's a much larger space here, far, far so, much larger than the meadows around Oxleisure Pool, far larger than those; several golf courses could easily fit in this "PRIVATE" parkland.

The sun is burning bright and clear now, chasing off the last of the mist. The road bends around a cricket pitch — a white pavilion on the far side of it, and, to the right, I see more lodges. A few deer over there, beside the cricket pitch; the first deer I've seen, the first animals besides birds ... I see a car on the move up ahead: Is it coming this way?

... No ... A couple now going the other way, and they must both have seen me, but neither seems to give a toss. From that distance, though, they can't see my face; I could be anyone, and that anyone is more likely to be someone who works on the estate than a random Brummie.

A gate now, and this one is shut; a black, iron gate, high and ornate and spiked on top. The gate is decorated with golden crowns, golden sheaves, golden Ws; and a blue-and-gold coat of arms with the words "*Virtus Non Stemma*" — Virtue Not Ancestry, the Grosvenor family motto. I push the gate, but it won't open; I fiddle with it, see if there's any latch, but there's not, so I take to the grass beside the gate, follow along the fence, see how far it goes, see if there's a better place to climb, somewhere further from the road — the road I've just seen three cars drive along. Twenty metres from the gate, the metal fence is only a bit over waist-high; I can climb that easily. I lob my bag over, then leap over myself.

Ah, here's another car now, and this one looks like it's coming for me ... Looks like there's a camera on top of it; a black Range Rover it is. Yeah, it's definitely coming for me ...

As I walk back onto and along the road, that car drives through the gate that I couldn't get through. It comes up behind, driving slowly ... Right behind me now, then along-side me ... "You ok?" he says, staying inside the car — a stocky middle-aged meathead with a crew cut; he wears black, has a body-cam on a stab vest.

"Yeah, good."

Then, oddly, he asks the same thing again: "You ok, yeah?"

"Yep." And I stick the dictaphone through the window. "Anything you say may be ..."

"Ok." And I expect him to maybe ask something, like, I don't know, what the heck I'm doing, but he doesn't ... He doesn't ask anything.

"Here's my card," I say, and I hand it through the window. "Yes, .schule, that *is* a German domain ..."

"Ok."

And that's it.

I carry on walking, and he hovers behind in the car.

As I stroll through the succulent parkland, I wonder why that bloke hasn't questioned me more — or, in fact, at all. I wonder if Dobbs put out a memo about me ... "NOTE: A prat has invited himself to visit us. Say nothing to this prat." As I ponder that, the guy drives past me and off down the road.

I see him again standing beside the gate that leads into the village of Eccleston. He's already opened the gate for me by the time I reach it. He doesn't say anything. I ask if Dobbs told him I was coming, but he says not; he doesn't even know who Dobbs is. I walk out, and he locks the gate after me.

PLAGUE-ENFORCED SABBATICAL

My fuel for being a protesting, annoying twerp this year is, I'm sure, related to my two-year plague-enforced sabbatical in a communist country, where I, nor anyone else, could be a protesting, annoying twerp.

So, what happened there in Laos?

I went to Thailand in late 2019 to do some promo for a book I'd just finished; the plan was to do that for half a year, then do a new book: Cairo to Cape Town was an option, as was an odyssey along the Zambezi.

In February 2020, I took a bus from Chiang Mai, in the north of Thailand, to Vientiane, the capital of Laos; then I headed four hours north to an off-grid paradise, Tao Guesthouse, really out in the sticks. China, by then, had shuttered several cities, but I didn't think much of it. I thought: Overreaction, authoritarianism on steroids.

What follows are excerpts from emails I sent:

30th March 2020: "The panic started to spread, and most tourists bolted home, even though there are no confirmed cases in Laos. The WHO said Europe is the new epicentre, so I thought there was no point returning to Birmingham. I came back to Tao Guesthouse, which, I thought, would be a good place to be in case Laos gets whacked into lockdown — which we have been now. Flights have stopped, and the land borders closed on March 22nd. (They gave less than 24 hours notice.) We're officially in lockdown, but way out here in the country-side, things are as before, and the lockdown isn't much of a lockdown. We can't go too far, can't travel elsewhere in the country, but we can stroll around this area. Still, we — sixteen people, all Europeans — don't go out much because the locals pinch their noses and hold their breath if we walk past them on the road — even if they're several metres from us. We don't have to leave the grounds of the guesthouse, really, as they grow their own food, and they sell Beer Lao for £1. We play Scrabble and Shithead; we swim in the river beside the guesthouse; yesterday, I went to a waterfall in the jungle ... I've no idea what's happening in the country beyond this bubble here. The local sources of information are the *Laotian Times* and the *Vientiane Times*, but all media here is moderated by the government (communists!), so who knows what's really going on. Locals know not to trust the news, so they rely on Facebook for "facts" ... Michele — the guesthouse owner, an Italian — is a full-on conspiracy crank. He was one before Covid — lizard rulers, 9/11 was the CIA, 5G is mind-control ... — and Covid has slammed him into overdrive: David Icke is right, he thinks, and nothing the BBC says is true. He claims *no one* is even in hospital, claims all that footage is fake ... I'm not on board with any of that. No, the world isn't controlled by a shadowy boardroom of depraved reptiles but rather by an uncoordinated cocktail of flawed

men, a mix of mainly pricks and idiots. Sure, they're self-
ish, but they're human. Trump is an awful twat but isn't a
lizard. Windows Vista did suck, but that doesn't make
Gates evil. When I told Michele that Gates is simply a
weird nerd, he said, "That's what he wants you to think!"

24th August 2020: I'm not in the countryside any more; I
was there for six weeks for the lockdown, and then I
came to the capital, Vientiane ... There are ten or so of us
at Syri Guesthouse, which is one of only a few
hotels/guesthouses still open ... Some strange characters
in Vientiane: There's a Kenyan who came to do a
marathon in the country but is now a pro meth junkie;
and there are a couple of Ukrainian hookers who had
been working in Myanmar and illegally crossed the
border into Laos; and there's an angry, shaggy Russian
who lives on the streets and films himself badly chatting
up passing women and then posts the videos on Facebook with horrific misogynistic comments ... The restaurants, markets, and bars are open, and few people wear
masks, and there's no social distancing, because the
government insists there's no Covid in Laos now. The
only thing closed are the borders and airports. From
here, I can *see* Thailand, a hundred metres across the
Mekong. There's a bridge from Vientiane to Nong Khai
on the other side, but no one's allowed to cross it. I've
considered sneaking into Thailand, as flights are running
from there, but though I reckon I could slip into the
country without issue, I'm sure they wouldn't let me
board a flight out if I don't have an entry stamp in my
passport. They'd work out from my Laos visa stamps
where I'd come from, and they'd work out that I'd ille-
gally crossed the border, and then ... well, they'd be

pissed. I'd probably be jailed for that. And I'd rather be stuck in Laos than stuck in prison in Thailand.

26th April 2021: I fancied a change of scene, so I came to Luang Prabang — a town in the north of Laos, about a nine-hour drive from the Thai border. Maybe I should have stayed by the border, but I waited in Vientiane beside it for *seven months*, and it didn't open for even *one day* ... I found a good room at Malida Guesthouse (where I'm the only guest), and it's wildly beautiful up here — the Mekong, the temples, the green. But now I can't enjoy the place, as we're in lockdown because of a few dozen Covid infections. After no new cases in the country for several months, Covid came back via Thailand, apparently; they're tracing it to a Laotian who went there and back on the sly to get a nose job — she's getting slaughtered in the press ... So now there's a curfew, and most roads are blocked off with homemade barriers manned by vigilantes, which means I can't walk far. And I have to wear a mask in the street — *outdoors*, for Christ's sake — which sucks when it's 35+ degrees. The road I live on may also be blocked starting tomorrow, and I may need "permission" to come and go. Not sure yet sure how strict it will be, but at least there's a shack shop on my road that sells pot noodles and biscuits and candy and fags. A shitty situation, and I can't escape elsewhere as travel to other provinces is blocked.

17th July 2021: We're out of total lockdown, but they keep extending the partial lockdown. Shops and restaurants are mostly open, but we can't go inside them; we instead have to stand outside and order what we want. Walking around the centre is fine, but most side roads are blocked.

No travel between provinces is allowed unless we've been double-jabbed *and* have written permission from the "Covid Taskforce" — and they don't give that permission unless the reason to travel is good; "I'm bored here": that's not a good enough reason ... I'm double-jabbed with Sinopharm, some Chinese poison. I didn't want it, but if I didn't have it, I'd have been booted out of this guest-house, and I wouldn't have been able to check into another guesthouse — what's left of them — as they all want proof of vaccination. Well, not *all* of them: Tao Guesthouse doesn't care, and Michele is holding firm on his no-vaccine policy. He still thinks the whole thing is a hoax, totally made up. He emailed me last week, actually, and said someone tried to steal one of his cows in the night, but he heard a noise and scared them off with a machete. He's barely had a guest in over a year. Up here, it's depressing to see all the "FOR SALE" signs on the hotels and restaurants and shops, to see the buildings deteriorating. There are no Covid handouts in Laos, no government cheques mailed out to make up for lost wages, so these lockdowns financially pummel people ... Vong, the owner of the guesthouse I'm at, is also a teacher, and she's rarely been paid by the school during Covid — the schools, by the way, have been closed for months, and there are no classes over Zoom.

16th October 2021: Back in proper lockdown. There were only 20-odd cases in the town (a town of 60,000 people), but that sent us back to supermarkets closed, and restaurants as well (even for take-out), and the town centre cordoned off. I've been off my road twice in two weeks — to go to the ATM and the pharmacy. God knows how long it will go on; it could easily be another month ... But at least I've got something to be getting on with: rewriting *Footloose*, my first book. Going through that book now, that overland journey from Sydney to London, it feels more like fiction than non-fiction ... I might be rewriting myself out of a chance of ever returning to Thailand, as the rewrite of that chapter has a chunk slating the Thai King, which is illegal there. Some Australian bloke wrote much less than what I have, and he was much more vague, and he got jailed for it ... No idea when I'll be back. The land borders haven't opened once since March 2020. Irregular — and extremely expensive — charter flights have left, but the paperwork and permissions are insane ("exit permission" is required from the authorities). The flights have to be booked weeks in advance and only via a local travel agent. Plus, I'd have to go via Korea — a twenty-hour layover — and then self-isolate in the UK, as Laos is on their "red list". A PCR test has to be done the day prior to the flight: If I fail that test, I'll be carted off to a "field hospital" for ten days, and having seen photos of those places (a hundred beds in a hangar), that would be shit. Not only will I be banged up in a hangar, I'll lose the cash for the flight, and I can't afford to lose that cash ... This Covid bullshit has been a disaster for my income: people can't travel, so aren't all that buzzed about reading about travelling, and I've drained the money I had left from when I sold that website a few years ago. I'm on the verge of being a monk for a while: I'd stop leaking money, and I'd maybe become enlightened — or, at least, less of an ass.

In the end, I got back to England — via Singapore and Germany — on March 9th 2022. Two years I was there, a place I planned to be at for two months; and it was almost, and I don't exaggerate, the end of me. If I were in England and slapped with *extreme* restrictions like I endured, I'd have said, "Screw this shit," and I'd have gotten on with life, risked arrest and whatever, rather than letting absurd decrees pulp me. I'd have worn a mask on a train or at the supermarket, but not much more than that.

In Laos, though, I was under the thumb of a communist government; I had to accept those severe diktats. I was infuriated, as, of course, the locals were: they were ordered to stay home and not work, yet they were given no handouts or support. No one dared slag off the puppet masters publicly. Any sort of protest was never on the cards; in somewhere like Laos, that would be brutally squashed; people would die. Freedom of speech, the right to protest: we have those in England; if we see something we don't think is right, we can do something about it. So that's why I'm being a protesting, annoying twerp this year — because I can be.

Two more reasons why that time in Laos ties into this and isn't just an off-piste rant ...

1) When I was at Tao Guesthouse before Covid, I roamed the countryside freely. In Laos, there's no concept of public footpaths or permissive footpaths; it's just accepted that anyone can walk anywhere so long as they're not damaging anything or intruding on privacy. That isn't a communist policy; that's Buddhism, if anything, though really more common sense.

2) Laos had a royal family until the communists rose up in 1975. The royals were arrested and packed off to labour camps, where most of them died. Lao's neighbour China and Lao's friend Russia both did the same: had revolutions that saw their royalty and aristocracy exterminated; in both instances, communism being the cause. I say this not

to advocate communism; I say this to show that disgruntled peasants have power and that royalty and aristocracy in England would be safer if they shared more of what they have. People shared with are less likely to anger and turn against the sharer.

France — which, for a while, colonised Laos — should also be a warning for the ultra-privileged aristocracy in England. The plebs in France got very angry indeed, and that turned out extremely badly for the French aristocracy ...

At the time of the French Revolution — 1789 — the estates of *la noblesse* comprised about one-fifth of the land. The poor, starving peasantry rebelled, and they started hanging aristocrats from lampposts. But there were so many aristocrats that they needed a more efficient method of murder, and some genius created the guillotine. Great crowds of spectators eagerly watched as bourgeoisie heads fell. Two days after the storming of the Bastille, the British Ambassador to France — the 3rd Duke of Dorset — reported to the Secretary of State for Foreign Affairs — the 5th Duke of Leeds — that, "From this moment, we may consider the French nobility reduced to the level of the rest of the nation." A few years later, King Louis XVI was guillotined, and Marie-Antoinette — "Let them eat cake!" — was guillotined, and the monarchy was abolished in France.

The Thai royals remain, and as I mentioned in one of the emails, you can't even *criticise* their King. That chapter rewrite didn't make it into the updated version of that book because I was, at that time, still hoping to cross from Laos into Thailand. And even after I returned to England, I had doubts about it: If I published what I wrote, I'd never be able to go to Thailand again; was it worth it?

No, I initially thought, but now ... Yes, now *is* the time, and *this* book is the place for it. So here's what I wrote about the Thai King ...

Section 112 of Thailand's Criminal Code quells any dissent against the monarchy. Truth isn't a defence. Harry Nicolaides, an Australian, was sent to jail in 2009 for writing one paragraph — 103 words! — deemed to be offensive to the monarchy. He wrote those words in a self-published novel, *Verisimilitude*. Fifty copies printed. Seven sold. At court, handcuffed and wearing heavy, rusted shackles, he was sentenced to three years. He was in a 12-by-5-metre cell with 50 other people, locked in there from 16:00 until 06:00. In that one-bog cell were rapists and murderers, as well the "Merchant of Death" — a Russian arms dealer — and a Canadian paedo known as "Swirl Face".

This precious monarch is Bhumibol, and he's deified by Thais. The longest reigning monarch in the world — sixty-plus years on the throne — is met with adoring crowds who prostrate before him and look up to him as a living Buddha. His portrait is displayed not only in businesses and restaurants and schools but very often in people's homes as well. When, in 2002, he published a book about his dog, it was a bestseller.

What a guy.

But then take *this* book as an example: imagine if it were illegal to write a bad review of it; imagine if giving it even 4 stars, not 5, would result in prison time. If that were the case, it's not hard to imagine its rating on Amazon would be 5/5, "Best book ever!". (When, by now, you've realised that it's more like 3/5.) So this King, who knows what to make of him ... He's 5/5, "Best King ever!", if you ask any Thai, but any Thai is scared shitless of saying anything else. And, anyway, they mostly only know the official propaganda drilled into them from when they're toddlers until they're pensioners. They're not told that declassified British and US diplomatic cables say that he's given his blessing to many of the coups that have crippled the country's democracy. They're not told that he's the world's richest monarch; that, in 2011, *Forbes* put his wealth in excess of £20 billion. Another thing they're not told are the details of the death of his older brother that resulted in Bhumibol taking the throne when he was 19 ...

In 1946, the 20-year-old brother of Bhumibol — Ananda, the King — was shot dead in his palace bedroom. Shot in the head with his own pistol, a bullet wound between his eyes. It was said, at first, to be an accident, Ananda playing around with his pistol. Then suicide was suggested. But a team of a dozen doctors ruled out a self-inflicted accident and also considered suicide highly unlikely. One of the doctors said: "The position of the wound and the bullet track seem to show that death was the result of assassination rather than suicide." That an unknown assassin sneaked into the Grand Palace that morning and managed to get into and out of Ananda's bedroom unseen was judged impossible. Plus, surely an assassin would take his own gun and not just hope that Ananda happened to have one on hand — "Excuse me, my King, but could I possibly borrow your pistol to shoot you with?" So it was ruled an inside job: Two servants were charged and executed for the murder of the King, even though the case against them was weak and the trial irregular — it was an on-off affair for seven years. Bhumibol could have commuted their sentences

— maybe life in prison because of the absence of any credible motive or evidence — but he didn't. The last person to see him alive, to see Ananda in his bedroom? His brother, Bhumibol, who said that he went into his brother's bedroom at 09:00 but left as his brother was asleep. 09:20 was when Ananda was shot. An accident, perhaps: Bhumibol not realising the pistol was loaded ... Or maybe on purpose: Bhumibol had a motive, after all — he was next in line to the throne. There's no evidence that Bhumibol murdered his brother, but there's no evidence because there was no investigation into Bhumibol. To suggest Bhumibol might have done it would have meant death for the person suggesting that possibility. If anyone in the palace had heard the gunshot and then seen Bhumibol fleeing the room, it's inconceivable they would testify that. But even then, there were whispers. Secret cables from the time — now available, though not in Thailand — show that the British and American Ambassadors believed, from speaking to people in the know, that it was Bhumibol to blame and there had been a deliberate cover-up. And Kenneth Landon, a Southeast Asia expert for the CIA, who spent a lot of time in Thailand in the forties and fifties, and who spoke fluent Thai, was in no doubt: Ananda was "killed by his brother, either intentionally or accidentally" he said, after he'd retired, when he was far away from Thailand.

Bhumibol might be 5/5, "Best King ever!", or he might be 1/5, "Politics-meddling murderer!", but no one can be sure because no one probes, no one rocks the tuk-tuk, because no one wants to go to jail.

As if they put up with that, you might think; *Jailed for criticising their King?! We'd never put up with that in this country;*

that's medieval nonsense. Yes, well, we might not put up with *that*, but we put up with the aristocracy bullshit — even Thailand has done away with that; they have a royal family but not layers of dukes and earls. And you can bet that people in other countries look at *this* country, look at England, and say, "So let me get this right: England has these dukes and barons and marquesses and viscounts and earls, and they own 25% of the land, even though there are less than 1,000 of them? And they won't even let the plebs *walk* on a lot of that land? And these dukes and barons and whatever, they only have that land because of nonsense from medieval times, like Henry VIII, William the Conquerer, that long ago? Ha! Idiots! As if they put up with *that*."

MAKE A DONATION

I'm *inside* Chatsworth House, home of the Duke of Devonshire. Not hundreds of metres away, far down his driveway, but actually inside. I'm nosing around, looking at his bits and bobs, his busts and paintings, his antique furnishings ... climbing his grandiose staircases, walking his floral-pattern carpeted corridors in my flip-flops. I see oak panelling — sourced from a German monastery — narwhal tusks, mural-painted ceilings, Damien Hirst art ... see the Great Chamber — its ceiling depicting Astraea, Goddess of Justice ... see 17th-century tapestries and Old Master drawings, see Chinese porcelain and Italian sculptures of mythological figures ... a 17,000-book library, portraits of ancestors — a lot named William Cavendish ...

I didn't come in through a window ... I came into this palatial, baroque mansion — part *Pride & Prejudice*, part Palace of Versailles — through a regal, gilded gate, under a high stone arch from which flies a black flag with three white stag heads on it, and I handed over £28 — just like the rest of the plebs in here. I was conflicted about paying to enter — paying £28 to Peregrine Cavendish, the 12th

Duke of Devonshire, a bloke 183rd on *The Sunday Times Rich List 2023* (£900 million) — but I wanted to see inside a whopping mansion like this: a place that makes Lord and Lady Barstow's residence appear small and dull.

The staff in the plush, florid rooms wear blue twill waistcoats with gleaming buttons, and they dash around stopping touchy Indians from touching things, and saying, "Excuse me, if you could, please, move on, please," to Chinese women blocking staircases with their non-stop selfie-taking, and telling Americans, "Please, could you, please, wear your rucksack on your front, please, if you wouldn't mind, please." Of the 300 or so rooms in the house, only 30 are open to visitors. The rest are where the duke lives. The rooms open aren't really used now; they're more like a museum, but there are a couple of exceptions: "The duke still uses this room?" I ask the young guide in the swanky dining room, where the long table is set — silver candelabra and glinting knives and forks.

"Yes, he does, for special occasions," she says, her Yorkshire accent still tinged with her native tongue — Hungarian, I'd guess. "He uses it about, maybe, five times a year."

"Can it be rented? Could *I* rent it?"

"You can, yes."

"Do you know how much it costs?"

"I don't, no, but it will be a lot. The Painted Hall, we had a wedding ceremony there last year — an American couple — and I heard they paid £50,000."

"Big money."

"It is, yes, and the charity needs it. We never have as much as we need. There are always unexpected things that come up — like, last year, during the heatwave, in one of the guest bedrooms, the Chinese hand-painted wallpaper started to peel off, so that's been a big cost to fix. And the

Cascade in the garden, that needs a lot of work — that's the next big project."

"The duke, though, he has that art collection, one of the most valuable in Europe; he could sell one or two of those paintings, right, say, one of his Rembrandts, to pay for this or that?"

"Hmm ... But the house is part of the trust. It's a difficult situation, I think. I don't know."

"The trust" ... "the charity" ... A sign by the entrance said, "We are very grateful that you have chosen to visit and support Chatsworth House Trust, a registered charity since 1981 ..."

I'll explain. It's a little complicated ...

This 35,000-acre estate — that's 20,000 football pitches — is legally owned by the Trustees of the Chatsworth Settlement on behalf of the Cavendish family, who bank the profits from it. That trust was set up in 1946 as a tax dodge — a tax dodge that, at first, went wrong due to an untimely death, but I'll come to that ... Then, in 1981, the Trustees of the Chatsworth Settlement created a charitable foundation, Chatsworth House Trust, for "the benefit of the public". The duke and his son are directors of Chatsworth House Trust, which was granted a 99-year lease of the house and its grounds and its parkland and forest — a total of 1,800 acres. It pays £1 a year for rent. The charitable income each year is about £15 million — sourced largely from visitor tickets to the house and garden — and is spent, after running costs, like staff wages, on house and grounds conservation and maintenance. So that £28 I've paid, and that all the other peasants stumped up, goes to looking after the duke's house — a house that he still has 90% of the rooms to live in.

This house and this charity have nothing to do with the

National Trust or the English Heritage Trust — the latter of those a charity that manages hundreds of historic places, like Stone Henge and Hadrian's Wall. An adult annual membership for the National Trust costs £84; for that, you get free entry to over 500 places ... One of which is Hardwick Hall, 30 km from here — Hardwick Hall that once belonged to the Dukes of Devonshire. The 11th duke handed it to the National Trust but not out of goodwill; it was because of that tax dodge that went wrong: 80% of the estate's value was owed in death duties to the government after the 10th duke died earlier than expected. The amount due was £7 million — £255 million in today's money. The 11th duke was screwed because he didn't have that much cash, so he had to start selling off land and offering up treasures, one of which was Hardwick Hall — he gave it to the government, the government gave it to the National Trust. The ~~shady~~ clever Trustees of the Chatsworth Settlement is there to prevent a repeat of that; it means minimal inheritance tax will ever have to be paid on this huge estate — which is only half of the Cavendish kingdom: there's also the 28,000-acre Bolton Abbey Estate, plus 8,000 acres in Lismore, Ireland.

Still, if you want to donate, here's the link: https://www.chatsworth.org/support-us/ (Make a one-off donation or pledge a monthly gift; your kindness today could help ~~save a child's life~~ save Peregrine spending his own money on his own house.)

In the garden now, which I enter via the orangery, passing by sculpted marble lions ... Large, green lawns; lakes and fountains; statues spread around. The house there: creamy-coloured, colossal, courtly, its window frames gilded in 24-carat gold leaf. I walk around, and I see Emperor Fountain — a jet of water shooting high, spraying mist onto the people lounging beside it. I see Victorian glasshouses, the rockery, the maze ... Then I lay down, try to catch a snooze, as I had to get up at 06:30 today to get here. I didn't arrive until 11:00 — the last 45 minutes of the journey on an old, red bus, the 218 from Sheffield Interchange to the Derbyshire Dales. Without a car or paying for a pricey hotel, it's hard to come here — unless you camp ... Easy to hide in here: hunker down at kick-out time (17:30), then set up camp after the final sweep is complete. Hide in the maze, for example: Are they going to comb every passage of the maze to check that no one is being a sneaky overstayer? No. A lot of great camping spots, if you go a bit off-piste, flat, woody, grassy spaces ... But I had to leave my bag in a locker outside — they don't allow larger rucksacks in the house — so I don't have my camping things with me. To camp in here, I'd have to leap the wall with my bag to come back in. How high is the wall? Not far off head-height, I saw from scouting the perimeter of the garden, with barbed wire along some of it. I won't bother doing that ... This is only 105 acres of the estate; there are plenty of other acres ...

I exit the garden, cross a three-arch bridge over the River Derwent, and I'm into the estate's parkland: absolutely massive, stretching for kilometres. Hundreds of sheep, hundreds and hundreds, scattered around — *baaaaaaaa*. I stroll around the parkland and through New Piece Wood and Maud's Plantation, browsing places to camp. Their website explicitly states, "No wild camping", but so what? I sent Peregrine the same email that I sent Hugh. The reply this time came from Chatsworth's PR company, from a woman called Lizzie — Director at Citypress ...

"... Camping is not permitted on the estate ... no exceptions are made to this policy ..."

I replied ...

"Thanks for the reply, but I think you might have misunderstood: I wasn't asking for permission; I was rather
informing you that I'm coming. The point of the book is
to draw attention to the large swathes of land unjustly
owned by dukes and to highlight that they have so much
land that they can't keep tabs on it all, and also to let
people know what — if anything — happens if they're
caught roaming and camping on that land. I'm coming,
and I'm writing a chapter about Chatsworth. That
chapter is happening, one way or another — if I'm frog-
marched off the estate, I'll write about that."

Lizzie didn't reply.

So I'll camp in this parkland if I want, even though they
have security here ... In the car park outside the entrance to
the house, I saw a white car labelled "SECURITY", which
had a yellow-and-blue police-like design on its sides. The
security, though, they'll likely just stick to the roads, one of
which passes through this parkland, but if I pitch up 100
metres from the road, they won't see me. A dark green tent
— like mine is — can't be seen at night. I've had it up in a
garden overnight, and I couldn't see it from the house
window, less than 20 metres away. At Hugh's estate, the
meathead wouldn't have seen me if I hadn't taken to the
road. The security here, walking around this parkland at
night? No, I don't see them doing that.

I cross the parkland to Edensor — which sounds like a planet in *Star Wars* but is a village owned by Peregrine: Genteel 19th-century cottages — with names like Hollybush and Church View — and a tearoom that sources ingredients from Ginger Butchers and Tomson Fruit & Veg. The village noticeboard displays posters: "Annual Shell Fayre — Cavendish Hall At Chatsworth — See & Buy Nature's Treasures From The Seven Seas". One lists the attractions for the upcoming Edensor Day: "Matthew & His Traditional Barrel Organ ... Powder Keg Morris Dancers ... Punch & Judy ... Quality Bric-a-Brac ... Wood Bodgers ..."

A half-deaf biddy starts a chat with me, poking her head over a rose bush she's trimming: "And what's your name?"

"Mark."

"Brian?"

"No, Mark."

"Oh, sorry, Matthew, sorry, my hearing isn't what it used to be. Are you here on holiday?"

"Yes."

"Are you staying in a sort of hostel place?"

"Something like that, yes."

By the bench in the village green is a box of books: *Where Is God In a Messed-Up World?* and *Christ, The Cross, And The Concrete Jungle* ... For kids, there's *Jesus The Storyteller* ... There's also *LIFE — A Christian Magazine*; one of the features is Let It Be, Protecting Our Bees, another is Top Picnic Tips; it also has puzzles. And, over there, is St Peter's Church — *Bong. Bong. Bong. Bong. Bong. Bong. Bong.* Most of the Dukes of Devonshire are buried in its graveyard, and I wonder, with tomorrow being Sunday, if the duke might go there, and if *he's* going there, if *I* should go too ... Not to egg him — "How do you like your eggs, Your

Grace, raw?" *SPLAT*. No, that would be inappropriate in a church, even for an atheist philistine like me. No, just *see* the man, *see* a duke face to face.

I've seen some clips of this duke online, videos where he's talking about Chatsworth. There was a clip where he was in the library there, and the interviewer asked how many he'd read, and he said not many of them, said he preferred comics. In another clip — from a 2012 BBC fly-on-the-wall documentary called *Chatsworth* — he was in a high-vis vest on his hands and knees in a hedge, fishing out a crisp packet, part of an estate litter pick. In an interview with *The Telegraph*, he said, "I don't like being called 'Your Grace.'" And he's quoted as saying in 2010 that he'd "be happy" to give up his title; he said he'd done nothing to earn it.

Cool. Sounds like a dude, not a duke.

But he's also said, "The aristocracy isn't dying, it's dead. It doesn't exist except that people have titles." Which isn't cool. A dick — that's what I thought when I read that. Sod the titles, which mean bugger all these days; the land — 25% of England — is where the aristocracy exists, and it's very, very much alive.

I leave Edensor and recross the river to see the parkland north of the Big House, beside 385-acre Stand Wood. There are sheep here, too, spread across the long, wild grass — *baaaaaaaa*. I see one black sheep — *black*. I thought they were like flying pigs, just something people said. Plenty of places in this vast space where I could stick up a tent: duck in by one of the many clusters of trees or up near Stand Wood — very difficult to be spotted there, well out of the way.

Stand Wood rises up a steep slope, and looking at it from here, I can see the Hunting Tower near the top, poking out above the trees. You can rent that tower; it has an Airbnb listing: £700 a night, with a minimum three-night stay. (An extra £35 per dog.) It dates from the 1500s when a long-ago Cavendish acquired this land. From their own website ...

> "William Cavendish prospered during the 16th century as one of Henry VIII's commissioners for the dissolution of the monasteries ... When he married Bess of Hardwick, she persuaded him to sell the former monastic lands he had amassed and move to Derbyshire ... In 1552, they began building Chatsworth ..."

"Prospered" from the dissolution of the monasteries: interesting choice of verb. One of the guides told me that the land was a "perk" of the job — a bonus for doing brutal Henry's wicked bidding. Henchmen is what the "commissioners" were, and "dissolution" is a fuzzy word for what was theft; for that's what happened: the lands of the monasteries were stolen, taken without payment and by force, taken and pocketed by Henry and his gang. This land I'm on now wasn't seized in the mugging of the monasteries, but Peregrine wouldn't have it now had his long-dead ancestor not thieved swathes of territory from monasteries. So "prospered" seems not quite right, does it?

Before I left the garden beside the house, I asked, all innocent, one of the staff, "So, err, what time does Stand Wood close?" And she said it doesn't close. It will be, I think, the place to camp; I prefer woodland to meadows ... I enter the woods and see there are arrowed routes, three to choose from, but I ignore these and head straight up the slope ... Pretty darn steep, and the sweat is streaming, and I'm puffing, huffing past a tall four-arch aqueduct, gasping

past a waterfall that cascades through boulders, until I
reach a plateau where there's a green lake, in which duck-
lings shadow their mother around. Maybe I'm trespassing,
maybe not: there's a footpath around the lake, but it's not
marked on the OS map, and there aren't any route arrows.
A field a little over there, through the woods and over a dry
stone wall, a field of chunky brown cows. No buildings
anywhere nearby. Squirrels around, but no people; I've not
seen a person since I entered these woods.

Security won't come up here. They won't walk these
woods all night on the off-chance someone is camping
here. I suspect, actually, they don't care all that much ...
The manager at Waddow Hall, which was where I camped
in Clitheroe, and which since 1927 has belonged to the Girl
Guides — there were *none* there when I was there; Z-E-R-O
— he told me: "We've got 198 acres here. We've got woodlands, and we've got footpaths, and in my experience,
trying to stop people doing things they shouldn't be doing
is more work than it's worth. Like, kids come down and
play on the weir; now, could we stop them? Yeah, potentially, but it's not worth our while, the manpower it would
take up. We put up a sign, but beyond that, we let it be."

And at the one monthly meeting at Huddleton Estate
that I did attend, cyclists on footpaths there was a point
raised: It wasn't that the Lord and Lady cared all that much
— *they* didn't have to walk on the paths — but they were
getting complaints from walkers, walkers saying they were
out on a chill stroll and amped-up cyclists were pelting
past them. It was discussed at that meeting a little, and the
conclusion was that nothing could be done. They'd put up
signs: "NO CYCLING"; what else could they do? Their
estate was just too darn large to police, and the Lord and
Lady knew it.

20:00 now, and I sit by the lake, enjoy the nature, the solitude ... A summer evening in the woods, that's when you really want to be here. The last bus has gone now — it left at 19:07. Even with a car, you wouldn't be able to be here now, as the car parks closed at 18:00. So wild camping here is the only way to experience this place at this time — unless you've £2,100 to spend on the Hunting Tower. I'm knackered: 32,000 steps today. It's one thing seeing these humungous estates on a map, but it's quite another when you're here on foot, mile after mile after mile ... then you *feel* the size of the land. I pitch up at sunset, a pretty spot a few metres from the lake, and I drop off a little after the last light fades to black.

I'm later woken by noise: Steps ... more steps ... coming this way ... a pause ... then steps again ... closer, closer, closer ... another pause ... then coming closer ... sneaky steps, some sly bugger creeping up on me ... A person or an animal? I can't tell, but if it's an animal, it's a hefty one, not a duck or a rabbit. There were wild hogs at Huddleton Estate, not the sort of beast you want to scrap with in the dark ... Mace, I need that mace, goddamn it, but I have nothing of the sort, no tool worthy of the name, nothing beyond my frankly feminine hands. I do the most manly cough I can muster, reach right down into the depths of my lungs and hack up a big-ass cough — the sort of cough I imagine a sumo wrestler coughing. Let this thing, this bastard or beast, know that I'm awake — and that I might be a blubbery Japanese man. This makes the thing pause, so I do it again, and then I hear the steps backing away from me, but the thing doesn't back off that far, doesn't leave the scene ...

My Mum told me to be careful on these trips, went on a worry tangent, said there are all sorts of weirdos and deviants and savages in this ugly world. I thought: She's got it the wrong way around: *It's safer out here* ... My parents had their cars robbed from their drive while they were upstairs asleep; some creeps broke in and nicked the keys. My sister, exactly the same thing happened: house broken into while she was sleeping, car stolen off her drive. A friend saw his insane neighbour batter a bloke to death with a pole, right outside his house; watched the foul scene out of his bedroom window. Just last week, three people in Nottingham — an hour's drive from here — were stabbed in the daytime by a random nutter. And, on the train here, I read in *The Metro*: "A Nazi sympathiser who built a submachine gun in his garage has been jailed for seven years ... He was preparing 'for a religious war', Birmingham crown court heard." This terror nearly always happens in towns and cities. In Manchester, on my way to Clitheroe, I had to change stations — Piccadilly to Victoria — and I walked through the middle of the city, past the Arndale shopping centre, which was bombed in 1996. Beside Victoria Station is Manchester Arena, which was bombed in 2017 — 500 injured, 22 killed. No one ever bombs the countryside, do they?

Now, after half an hour, I let myself drift back to sleep, telling myself: If the thing attacks, I'll wake up and be alert for it. I won't just awake in the morning with my face chewed off by a feral hog or awake with an abused rectum — "Jesus! Some filthy wrong 'un has bloody bummed me." I won't sleep right through the awful affair. No, I'll hear the thing come even if I'm asleep, then, in a crazed second, I'll spring into vicious action: blind it with Bleu de Chanel, spray that sweet scent right in its damn eyes, then shove nicotine lozenge after nicotine lozenge down its throat, poison the fucker.

THE ABBOT'S OAK

The narrator: "Down in his estate office, a bitter blow for Harold Avis. There's news which he believes could have devastating implications for the future of the Woburn Estate."

And there's grumpy Harold at his desk, an open news-paper in front of him, an ashtray beside the newspaper. He's the Estate Manager, about sixty years old; thickset and heavy jowls and a turkey neck.

A man behind the camera asks, "Why are you so angry, Harold?"

He sighs. "This new government plan to expand Milton Keynes: It's going to come totally on the edge of the estate."

"How many houses do they want to build?"

"25,000." Harold stands up and turns to face a large map on the wall. He points with a pen. "Milton Keynes is over here" — he points to the top left of the map — "and this is the border of the estate" — he runs his pen over the north-western boundary. He then points to Woburn Abbey in the middle of the map. "This is the Abbey" — he runs his pen from Woburn Abbey to just north of Aspley Guise, eight-ish kilometres away — "and that's where the houses are going to be." He then circles a broad region around Woburn Abbey. "This is the most beautiful part of Bedfordshire, and there's only one reason for that: because it belongs to the estate." He pauses, then says, "If they build 25,000 new houses, and there are four people to a house, that's 100,000 people dumped on this doorstep."

"So you're not a happy man?"

"Not a happy man at all."

"What will the Lord and Lady make of this?"

"They will be quite horrified."

It cuts to a sour-faced Lady Tavistock — daughter-in-law of the duke then, mother of the duke now. She's sat in her lavish living room in her 100-room house on her 13,000-acre estate; a white-gloved butler faffs about in the background. "It's very sad," she says. "But what can one do? Nothing."

We see the view from the window — expansive green, grass and trees and lakes — then the man behind the camera asks her, "Are you worried the estate will be swamped by townies?"

"Everyone is going to think, Oh, we'll go for a walk at Woburn, and that will impact us very badly. Why should we become like a public park?"

This is from *Country House*, a BBC2 documentary — three series, twenty-nine episodes — screened from 1999 to 2002. It was filmed entirely on the Woburn Estate. In another scene, Harold — wax coat, flat cap — is furious about a plastic bottle someone's dropped: "They live in bloody pigsties, I think, most of them. Though, that's being unkind to pigs."

I was the townie swine they feared: In the mid-nineties, I lived for two years right on the fringe of their estate (though, at that time, I didn't know it was their estate). I was a kid, so I was a mere piglet. I was a good piglet; I had a misspent youth, but at that point, I hadn't started misspending it ... that would come later. Now, they should fear me: I'm a full-grown rabid boar, and I'm back.

When I saw Harold fuming about that housing development, I thought: Nice one, Harold, for outlining the boundary of the estate, which until then I didn't know. Dukes are very darn secretive about their estate maps — they never put them on their websites — but Harold stupidly showed theirs on national television. I thought: I'll start there, at those woods in the north-west of their land, near Bow Brickhill.

In the woods — earthy and vibrant from recent rains — I come to a sign: "Aspley Woods is a large area of woodland owned by the Trustees of The Bedford Estates ..." *The Trustees of The Bedford Estates*: aka Andrew Russell, aka the 15th Duke of Bedford, aka the man 221st on *The Sunday Times* Rich List 2023 (£780 million). The Greensand Trust — an independent environmental charity — "manages public access" to the woods. Access? *Great!* Nothing to moan about here, right? But ... Aside from the access being sparse footpaths — and straying off those footpaths being trespassing — it's an "access agreement" which can be revoked whenever, and any time Andrew wants to turn parts of these woods into, say, a golf course, he can do. *He wouldn't do that! He wouldn't chainsaw woodland for a golf course!* Well, he did before ...

He did that *here*. Of that course — the 200-acre Marquess Course — *Golf Monthly* says it "... offers a tremendous expedition through mature woodland ... winding its way through a vast acreage of glorious countryside ..."

He did that, and his father did it twice before him in the 1970s — The Dukes Course, The Duchess Course.

I see the golf courses — all three of them — as I walk through the woodland that remains, walk among oaks, pines, birches, chestnuts; I see the emerald fairways, the velvet greens, see the wealthy in their yellow trousers and pink polo shirts and Ralph Lauren baseball caps, see them ambling around heavenly landscape, hundreds and hundreds of acres that you and I can't access unless we stump up £242 for a "game". It's a ruse, really, exclusion dressed as a game. It's not a game, not really: 1% of the time is hitting the ball, the other 99% is a stroll.

I don't stomp down the fairways; that would be aggravated trespass, would be "disrupting lawful activity" ... and I might get whacked by a ball, which would be embarrassing: "I declare my right to roam on this fairway, which is unjustly owned by the Duke of Bedford, and you can't stop me, you won't force me to leave, never. I'll stay, stay as long as I wa—*arghhhhhhh*."

I could camp here, though, in this woodland beside and around the greens and fairways, in, say, Bell's Copse or Little Brickhill Copse or Bow Brickhill Heath. No one golfs in the dark; to pitch up at sunset would be alright. But sunset is a long way off, and so too is Woburn Abbey — the head of the Bedford octopus — which is still miles from here, miles entirely through Andrew-owned land.

Through Charle Wood — ideal for camping — through seas of wheat undulating smoothly with the breeze, through wild fields of long grass and butterflies, and I come to a pretty village: Woburn: Red and blue doors and radiant hanging baskets; pricey, flowery dresses in the windows of Berchielli Boutique; an "art gallery by day, lounge bar by night" called Mosaic.

Woburn Heritage Centre is inside Old St Mary's Church on Bedford Street: There's an elderly bloke here, Simon, a volunteer at the centre for eleven years. We talk a little history, and then I ask: "What do people in Woburn think of the duke?"

"Well ... err ... everyone has different opinions."

"And your opinion?"

"I think His Grace ... I think he's an okay guy."

"You've met him?"

"Once I did, yes. I was in the car park here one day with my wife, and we were putting on our wellies, and this gentleman was walking past, and he said, 'Good morning,' and I said, 'Good morning,' and then I realised who it was, and I thought what a jolly nice chap, taking the time to say that to me."

"Did you watch that *Country House* program about the family? I saw some of the episodes on YouTube last week."

"I didn't see it at the time, no, but I know it was quite a notorious thing back then. I heard a lady, one of the estate staff, posed nude in it — nude! It's on YouTube, is it? I must check that out."

"The current duke, it's got his father in it — Lord Tavistock — the one who had a stroke when he was 48, but the actual duke at that time, the 13th one, he isn't in it."

"Yes, well, he was in Monte Carlo by then; he was a tax exile."

I tell him I'm here for a book I'm writing, and he says, "You'll go and introduce yourself at Woburn Abbey?"

"I sent them an email to say I'm coming, but they didn't like that email, so I'll just wander around uninvited."

"They do have footpaths there."

"The thing is, they have a couple of footpaths through the grounds, I know, because I've scouted them on the OS map, and, sure, that's better than nothing at all, but it's not much, is it? Those footpaths are, like, 0.1% of the estate."

"It's not much, no, and you do have to stick to the paths there; they're strict about that. They have rangers, and they really make sure you keep to the path; they sit in their Land Rovers up on the hill near the house, and they look out their binoculars for anyone that strays off the path. Yes, they're very, very strict about that."

I know that already, actually, as I read the recent Trip-Advisor reviews; these are some of them ...

> **Lee B:** "... having rangers drive at you from their little spot by the hill to tell people off like they're naughty children because they strayed slightly from the path is ridiculous."

> **Juiceylucey:** "An extremely loud, rude park ranger drove up to us and started to shout through his window at us to 'get back on the footpath' ... After this, the ranger sat in his Land Rover Defender watching us, revving his engine, then followed us to check we were doing what he had noisily said."

> **Jordan:** "The park ranger is very rude in telling people where they can and can't walk ... extremely petty stick to the path rule ..."

> **Arthur:** "The park ranger was rude in telling us to stick to the path (we were only cutting a corner). A polite reminder would of done fine, but the man's attitude was appalling."

I walk along Bedford Street, past a tailors called Souster & Hicks, and I turn right, and I'm soon outside the

Bedlin Wall — as I'll name it. At Whitewell, I made a quip about the gate I leapt into the "PRIVATE FISHING" place: "It's not exactly the Berlin Wall, is it?" Well, this wall here, this *is* like the Berlin Wall. This wall is three bricks thick and three metres tall. It's length: fifteen kilometres. F-I-F-T-E-E-N!!! That's how much wall it takes to seal off the 3,000 acres around Woburn Abbey.

I walk beside the Bedlin Wall for a mile and come to Crawley Lodge, where there's a gate to enter the grounds. A sign says, "KEEP TO THE PUBLIC FOOTPATHS — ALL OTHER AREAS ARE PRIVATE". I roam through Dean Hills — thick with trees and alive with birds — and then Sandylane Plantation and Brickground Plantation, where to vanish is easy; thirty seconds off the footpath, I'm absorbed by gorgeous forest.

I pass Trussler's Lodge into open pasture, grassland ... To the right, behind triple-layered chainlink fencing topped with barbed wire, is Woburn Safari Park: I see Fords and Nissans and Vauxhalls snaking around the prison camp of lions and rhinos and elephants. They offer a "VIP Safari Off-Road Adventure" for £375: "This amazing 90-minute tour takes guests through Savannah Grasslands, Kingdom of Carnivores, and African Forest ... You'll be taken incredibly close to the animals!" There are "more than 1,000 wild animals" in that 360-acre safari park; by comparison, the golf courses consume 600 or so acres. The manicured garden behind the Abbey, Andrew has 28 acres there: that's more space than the tigers at the safari park have (9 acres), more space than is given to the giraffes (9 acres) or the bears (13 acres — which they share with the wolves).

Since passing Trussler's Lodge, I've been in what they call the "DEER RESERVE" — frequent signs yell, "DEER

RESERVE — STAY ON THE FOOTPATH". I see the deer, as well as rabbits and squirrels. A lot of trees, and once I cross the road that runs through the middle of the "DEER RESERVE", I see many ponds too: Shoulder of Mutton Pond, Duncombe's Breeches Pond, Charcoal Pond ... Idyllic, ideal for a walk, and that's all you can do: walk. Sit? No. No benches anywhere, and if you sit on the grass, you're trespassing — anywhere not on the footpath is the "DEER RESERVE".

I see a white Land Rover parked on a hill, facing down the slope to the path, on the lookout — that's the spot referred to in the TripAdvisor reviews, and which Simon also mentioned; that's their surveillance headquarters, from where, with binoculars, they scour for criminals veering off the path. I'll be smart: I'll opt for chess, not boxing, *for now* ... No need *yet* for a seriously aggressive manoeuvre, a declaration of outright, screw-you war.

But I will go see that bloke there — see him and speak to him. I have questions ... questions about deer. I also want to see what he can see from up there, check the field of vision, the angles.

I walk up to him on the footpath, and through the window, I say, "Can I ask you a couple of questions?"

He doesn't answer, so I just start asking: "How many species of deer are there here?"

"Eight."

"And how many of those eight also live in the wild? Because there are six species of wild deer in the UK, and I'm wondering how many of those species you're keeping here in this — as you call it — reserve."

"I don't know how many species of deer live wild in the UK. I don't know about that."

Hmm ... It seems I know more about deer than he does,

which is strange because he's a ranger in a "DEER RESERVE", while all I know about deer I learnt from Wikipedia yesterday.

He doesn't seem to like talking about deer, so I change the topic: "Can you tell me where the Abbot's Oak is?"

"It's in the private area."

"It's by the bridge over there, by Basin Pond?"

"I'm not telling you. I know who you are."

"Word got around, did it?"

"Of course it has."

"So—"

"I'm not answering any more of your questions."

"But—"

"I'm not answering any more of your questions."

"Ok, well, I'll be around all day, and I'm camping here tonight, so come find me later if you change your mind."

"Camping?"

"Yeah."

"Where are you camping?"

"I'm not answering any more of your questions."

He knows who I am because I sent an email — "I accept my invitation to visit you ..." — and they replied ...

"... Working estate ... blah, blah, blah ... not permitted to leave the footpaths ... blah, blah, blah ... we do not permit camping ... blah, blah, blah ..."

Then I sent them: "Thanks for the reply, but I think you might have misunderstood: I wasn't asking for permission ..."

And, like Lizzie, they didn't respond.

How far, I wonder, did word get around? That grunt knows about my email ... did it go all the way to the top, to the duke? Did a white-gloved butler walk into that lavish living room in that 100-room house and say, "Your Grace ... err ... we've had an ... erm ... email."

"Yes? Spit it out."

"A man says he's writing a book called *Duchyland*, and he says he's going to camp here, and, well, he says he's not going to be a nuisance, but I think it's obvious, really quite clear, Your Grace, that he's a good-for-nothing rapscallion."

"Shoot the bugger! What do you think I'm paying you for?!"

I suspect that grunt knows more about deer than he let on, but he understood where my questioning was leading ... I'll come back to the deer, but I'll first deal with the Abbot's Oak: He knows why I was asking about *that* tree, that specific tree out of all the trees here, and I'm sure he knows the awful story about that tree, a very nasty story ...

Robert Hobbes, the abbot of Woburn Abbey — a former Catholic monastery — was one of those people who, after the Act of Supremacy in 1534, couldn't accept that the Pope was a turd. The Abbey was founded here in 1145, and for all that time, until 1534 — nearly 400 years — the Pope was the highest religious authority, but now that wasn't the case; now Henry VIII was the highest religious authority because Henry said he was. How to deal with that? It was like being told that, no, the sky isn't blue any more; it's actually orange. Why? Because Henry said so. The thing was if you didn't agree to the change — "No, Henry; *you're* a turd, and the sky *is* blue." — you were charged with treason, and the punishment for treason was to be hung, drawn, and quartered. This, in 1538, was the fate of poor Hobbes ... Hobbes, at trial, was found guilty of treason. He pleaded for mercy — "You know, you're right, the Pope *is* a turd." — but it was too late ... Tied to a horse, he was dragged through Woburn to the gallows: an old oak tree outside the Abbey. He was hung until he was almost dead, then he was sliced open and had his intestines ripped out, and his cock cut off, and had those bloody pieces burnt in front of him. He was then quartered: each of his limbs roped to a different horse, which rode off. His severed limbs and his hacked-off head were then nailed around Woburn as a warning to others.

With Hobbes gone, the Abbey was confiscated — the building and the land owned by the monastery. By 1540, 800 or so monasteries had been "dissolved", and that was a loss to the plebs as well as the monks, as those monasteries were much more than religious abodes; they were community centres, really, social services, society's safety net: they fed the poor and cared for widows, they educated orphans and nursed the sick ... pilgrims and passing travellers could sleep a night or two. The lands of the squashed monasteries were distributed to those who supported psycho Henry. John Russell — soon to be Earl of Bedford — was a cheerleader for Henry and was rewarded with this estate. He got not just this land but also land in Devon and London. The duke thing for the Russells came in 1694 — 1st Duke of Bedford! — the same year as the then Earl of Devonshire (William Cavendish) became 1st Duke of Devonshire, after the so-called Glorious Revolution, a revolution the two earls played a heavy hand in, a revolution that saw William of Orange depose James II as monarch. That's why Andrew today is Duke of Bedford and has all this land: Because one ancestor supported a vicious tyrant who hung monks from trees, and another ancestor supported a revolution to dethrone a lawful king. That's why today Andrew is "His Grace", and that's why today Andrew's grunts get to tell you where you can and can't walk.

The grunt wouldn't tell me where the Abbot's Oak is, but Google does ... The Bedfordshire Archives by Bedford Borough Council quotes the Royal Historical Society: "... an oak tree in sight of the Abbey, 193 yards from the south-west corner of the west front ..." I also find a detailed drawing of it by Jacob George Strutt, from 1822, called *The Abbot's Oak At Woburn*, which shows it close to a pond. So I go see the tree, go touch that gnarled, ancient oak, despite it being off the path — "PRIVATE AREA: NO PUBLIC ACCESS". In homage to Hobbes, I could claim, but really just as a fuck-you to Andrew and his grunts.

Now, deer ... this 2,500-acre "DEER RESERVE". That's not a thing; that's no more a thing than a "SQUIRREL RESERVE" or a "PIGEON SANCTUARY" or a "FOX REFUGE". Chatsworth House had deer; I saw them there in the park. I saw them, too, at Whitewell, roaming free, as I did at Huddleton Estate. London's Richmond Park is 2,500 acres, and 600 deer roam there — roam around the wandering, picnicking public.

The RSPCA's website says, "There are over a million deer living in the UK," and the Countryside Alliance says we have more deer "than at any time since the Norman Conquest". So we have a lot of deer — too many deer; so many, indeed, that the Countryside Alliance says, "They have a huge impact on other species, as well as the biodiversity of our environment." About this, there's an interesting *Independent* article from 2005 ...

"**The Silent Killer**: Britain's woodlands are being destroyed by a tiny breed of deer ... shaped like a pig, with antlers like salad tools. This is the muntjac — Britain's fastest-spreading wild animal — descended from a few animals that escaped from Woburn Abbey in

Bedfordshire a hundred years ago ... A recent census by the Mammal Society estimated that Britain is now home to at least 100,000 muntjacs, three times as many as 10 years ago."

Dear, oh dear: "... descended from a few animals that escaped from Woburn Abbey ..."

We have too many deer in the wild, and five of the six species in the wild they keep here in their "DEER RESERVE" — five out of their eight species. And the other three species, whatever they might be, surely they'd thrive in the wild as well, if given the chance, prosper as well as the five species that have shagged themselves into the millions. So, I wonder, is their "DEER RESERVE" deershit? It lets them say, "We would, of course, love to let you roam everywhere around the estate and not have to be petty about sticking to the footpath, but, unfortunately, we can't because of the deer, and you do love deer, don't you? You wouldn't want to do anything to harm the deer, would you? No, I thought not. So, therefore, stick to the bloody footpath."

Very clever branding by them to call it a "DEER RESERVE", very clever indeed. But the clever branding buckles when you hear that *they kill deer* — kill deer in *this* "DEER RESERVE" ... They kill deer — they brand that as a "cull" — and they also let rich people murder deer here ...

The Guardian, 2018: "Many Britons probably think that trophy hunting is something that happens abroad. But anyone looking to bag an animal's head to grace that empty spot on their wall needs only to head to deepest, darkest Bedfordshire ... A red deer stag, highly prized by hunters because of its magnificent antlers, can be shot for

a £9,000 trophy fee, according to an online price list
dated 2018 and distributed by a Danish travel company
called Limpopo & Diana Hunting Tours. The company
has been offering clients a range of shooting packages in
Bedfordshire, including some at Woburn Abbey ...
'Woburn Abbey is ideal for this, and we can do Père
David and red stag as well,' the company's sales director
explained ..."

The estate didn't deny it at the time, and they wouldn't
address questions about it.

If they allow cars to drive through the "DEER
RESERVE" — 19 killed last year by cars, 9 so far this year, a
sign I saw by the road said — and if they allow wealthy
hunters to shoot the deer — "That will be £9,000, please."
— then I'm allowing myself to camp in the "DEER
RESERVE".

I wait for the cloak of dusk, then I walk to Lower Hop
Garden Pond, to a clump of trees by it. The tent is up in
under five minutes, and once in it, I'm near-invisible —
more than 100 metres from any footpath or road, more
than 100 metres from any building. I'm 99% sure I'll be
alright here — though they do have security at night: I
know because I Googled "Woburn Abbey Security" and
found a listing on a job site ...

"... Shift work is required. The rota is based on a 4-on-4-
off basis, including night shifts and weekends ..."

I saw the LinkedIn profile for one of their current
"Security Officers": Ten months he's worked on this estate;
prior to that, for five years, he was Assistant Manager at

Pets At Home. So they have security, but it's not exactly A*
elite, is it?

The Abbot's Oak is near; if it's haunted, I'll hear the
cries, the moans, the hellish suffering of doomed Hobbes
485 years ago — "Hang him! Cut off his cock!" As I lay snug
in my little, green cocoon on ~~His Grace's~~ Andrew's ~~hard-
earned~~ unpaid-for 13,000-acre estate, I wonder: How about
another dissolution? The dissolution of the aristocracy.
Requisition their lands, hand them to ... I don't know ...
maybe the National Trust. Another revolution, too, if we
must, if the aristocracy is stubborn to change: Depose
Charles III and replace him with ... maybe no one? If there
were another dissolution, another revolution, well, so
what? The only real losers would be people who benefitted
from previous ones. We don't have to go total 16th century,
slice off Andrew's wiener ... No, we're more civilised than
that now — some of us, anyway; some still live in bloody
pigsties.

MONOPOLISED

Outside the station is a green, two-man tent quite similar to mine. The tent looks like it's been here a while; not hours but days — it has a dug-in look to it, a look of quasi-permanence. I walk past it and cross Euston Road onto Upper Woburn Place, and I walk that street through Bloomsbury, red buses driving by — the No.91 to Trafalgar Square, the No.168 to Old Kent Road ... I pass Woburn Walk, which leads onto Duke's Road, and I come to Tavistock Square, where, in 2005, a double-decker was bombed; four suicide bombers struck London that July day — 52 killed, 770 injured. A leafy park is within Tavistock Square: Opposite a cherry tree — "Planted in Memory of the Victims of Hiroshima." — sits a woman on a bench, eating a salad while reading a Javanese phrasebook, and in the park's centre is a bronze statue of a cross-legged, contemplative Gandhi, beside which a child in a pink tutu and heart-shaped glasses is posing for a photo. Gandhi studied law near here for a few years before returning to India to reclaim his nation's land. His strategy: civil disobedience:

refusal to comply with unjust laws. He saw that so few British couldn't, in practice, control so many Indians.

Woburn Place and Tavistock Place lead off Tavistock Square — Vladimir Ilyich Ulyanov lived on the latter of those roads for a year; Lenin, as he was better known, the architect of the revolution that binned Russia's nobility ... Bedford Way also runs off Tavistock Square and it stretches to Russell Square, where workmen in hi-vis yellow jackets lounge on the grass, tapping their phones, and an American student is ranting about how disgusting baked beans are: "I can't believe they eat that! I mean, for breakfast! *Really?!*" There's a pompous statue of Francis Russell, the 5th Duke of Bedford. There's no statue of illustrious suffragette Emmeline Pankhurst, who lived at No.8 Russell Square for a while. "Deeds, not words," was her motto, and in her forty-year campaign, she was imprisoned several times. The year she died, 1928, women were finally granted equal voting rights with men. In the corner of the park is a display detailing its history: "... In the 1500s, during the dissolution of the monasteries, Bloomsbury was seized by the crown and granted to the 1st Earl of Southampton, a loyal counsellor of Henry VIII ... The daughter of the 4th Earl of Southampton married William Russell, son and heir to the 5th Earl of Bedford, bringing Bloomsbury into the Russell family ..." At the bottom of the display, in small print, it says the park in Russell Square is "leased by The Bedford Estates to Camden Council". The Bedford Estates website skips over how they acquired this land — for free! — but says they've owned "much of Bloomsbury since 1669".

A street away from Russell Square is Bedford Square: Elegant houses and embellished lampposts around another lovely park. There's *no one* in this park, this park that's enclosed by black railings and locked gates with signs that state it's "PRIVATE". This park is only for those with a key — those with a key and those who know that trespass is basically bollocks. Other signs say, "These gardens are regularly patrolled by security personnel", but I don't see any, and I'm not worried about someone phoning the police ...

"Officer, there's a man in the garden!"

"A burglar in your garden, madam?"

"Not my garden, exactly."

"Your neighbour's garden?"

"No, it's a shared garden in the middle of the square."

"This shared garden, it's not attached to anyone's house? That sounds like a park."

"Yes, it is a park, really, but we like to call it a garden. The point, though, is that it's a *private* park, just for *us*."

"Ok. Well, this burglar, what's he stealing from this park?"

"He's not a burglar, actually; he's not stealing anything."

"What's he damaging?"

"He's not damaging anything."

"So what's he doing?"

"He's sitting on the grass, enjoying himself."

"Enjoying himself? You mean he's masturbating?"

"No. He's eating."

"Eating magic mushrooms?"

"No. A meal deal — not one from Waitrose, or even M&S, but from one of the peasant places: Tesco."

"Look, we can't really do anything about that. It's not a criminal offence, for starters, and we're also kind of busy with, you know, actual criminal offences. I'll put it on our to-do list, but it will likely be hours before we can get an officer there to check on this man eating a meal deal in a park."

"*Hours?!* But that's too long! He'll probably leave after he's eaten his meal deal."

"If he leaves after he's eaten his meal deal, what are you worried about? Bye."

All the parks in Bloomsbury were "PRIVATE" and locked until WWII when the iron railings and gates that kept out the plebs were removed and melted — by order of the government — to be used for making munitions. After the war, after hundreds of thousands of English working class had died defending England, someone at The Bedford Estates noted that putting all the iron railings and locked gates and "PRIVATE" signs back again to exclude the peasants looked pretty bad; after all, if the paupers hadn't risked their lives, the parks in Bloomsbury would all say, "*PRIVATGRUNDSTÜCK*". So the poor unwashed were allowed in *some* of the parks.

Montague Street links Russell Square with Great Russell Street, and on Montague Street are three grand trees in front of a tall ivy-covered brick wall; in the wall is a low-key royal blue door, a shiny brass plaque beside it: "The Bedford Estates". A very discreet headquarters for the cartel that controls Bloomsbury for Andrew while he chills on his 13,000-acre estate at Woburn.

An eight-minute walk from The Bedford Estates HQ is Covent Garden: Outside there, a crowd watch a bald, bulge-eyed man in a kilt: He has a three-metre ladder. The ladder isn't against a wall, but he climbs it; he climbs it and stays up there, using the ladder as stilts. "No hands!" he cries to the clapping crowd. He's up there ages, arsing around and bantering, then he whips off his kilt and shirt. In his boxers, his pot belly and moobs wobbling, high up the ladder that's leaning on nothing, he starts juggling knives ... Above the pillared entrance to Covent Garden, engraved in the yellowy stone, is a coat of arms: a crown and three escallops above a lion — the Duke of Bedford's coat of arms. The Russell family don't own Covent Garden now, but they did from Henry VIII's divorce tantrum until 1918. They sold it for £2 million — £2 million in 1918 is £300 million in today's money. A fine fortune for land that cost them nothing.

Like dogs pissing on trees, the Russells marked their territory at Covent Garden too: there's Russell Street, Bedford Street, Bedford Court, Bedfordbury ... I walk down Tavistock Court onto Tavistock Street, and, from there, I see a dark, faded, square plaque on the rear of the Lyceum Theatre: on the plaque are three lions and some text: "DUCHY OF LANCASTER". The theatre is on the Strand, which is heaving: Busy, striding people; a tour group of teenage Italians, all with orange backpacks; a beggar slouched outside Tesco Express, hand up for coins; cranks shouting about this, weirdos demanding that: "Free Assange!" ... "Save the pandas!" ... "You're going to hell!" ... A red tent across the road from Superdrug; and near Coutts — bank for the royals and aristocracy — a little grey tent: the door is open, and I see a woman asleep inside, see her pillow and duvet — a kid's design with unicorns and clouds.

The Savoy Estate is the jewel in the urban crown of the Duchy of Lancaster, and it's here ... but where, exactly? I emailed them to ask what is and isn't in this estate, and even suggested a meeting, as their head office is here, but they weren't helpful: They said, "I'm afraid that our Head of Communications is away on leave this week." They recommended I buy a dull book, *The Savoy: Manor, Hospi-*

tal, Chapel — a book published in 1960 by someone who worked for the Duchy of Lancaster. I didn't buy it. I did, though, scour the "Latest News" articles on their website, and they mention in one article — about a new tenant of theirs that sells Taiwanese bubble tea — that this estate extends "from the Strand in the north to the Embankment in the south and from the Savoy Hotel in the west to Somerset House in the east". As I walk around that area, I see "Savoy" in a lot of road names: Savoy Street, Savoy Way, Savoy Place ... and there are buildings with "Savoy" in their name: Savoy Hill House, SavoyStrand ... and a building named Duchy House — a building that has the Duchy shield engraved on its facade, as well as some text: "Nothing Without Labour". Plus, there are those square plaques that say "DUCHY OF LANCASTER", though I only find two more of those. Their website, of course, lists their own address: 1 Lancaster Place, which is in a huge art deco building that looks more suited to New York than London; from that building vainly flies a large Duchy flag — red with three gold lions.

The Duchy's website calls the Strand "one of London's busiest commercial streets". The shops and companies renting here — like Pret a Manger and Specsavers and CVC Capital Partners (a private equity firm) — will each be paying hundreds of thousands annually; cash pouring into the Duchy, year after year, decade after decade, century after century ... A massive, meaty cash cow. Rent out land acquired for bugger all — that's a great business ... and it's even better if you don't pay corporation tax nor capital gains tax, which the Duchy of Lancaster doesn't — nor does the Duchy of Cornwall. Of this year's profits, £19.5 million — 75% — came from their commercial property portfolio, which I know because last week they published their annual report for the past year. The total profit: £26.2 million — a £2.2 million rise on the year before and up 30% since 2018. That profit is Charles's, and that's on top of the £86 million Sovereign Grant — which, it was this week reported, is expected to rise to £125 million by 2025.

The rear of SavoyStrand overlooks The King's Chapel of the Savoy — a centuries-old church with a jazzy blue ceiling and flashy stained glass windows. The chaplain is inside, a tall, white-haired bloke in thick-rimmed glasses; on his black blazer is a lapel badge branded with the Duchy shield. I tell him I'm writing a book about land owned by dukes and that I've come to see what the Savoy Estate looks like.

"Ah, yes, this chapel is owned by the Duke of Lancaster."

"Does anyone call him that?

"Well, on Sunday mornings, we sing, 'God save our gracious King, long live our noble Duke'."

"Does he come here? This is his regular?"

"He hasn't come since he's been King, but before that, he came sometimes. If he's in London, he'll more likely go to the chapel at St James's Palace. But he's not often in London on a Sunday. He's at one of his other homes in Windsor or Gloucestershire or Norfolk or Scotland."

A sign outside says, "This chapel is the last surviving building of a hospital founded in 1512 for the 'poore and needye'." I mention that to the chaplain, and he says, "Yes, after the palace that was here — the Savoy Palace that the 1st Duke of Lancaster built — after that was destroyed in the Peasants' Revolt of 1381, a hospital was built here, and this chapel is the only bit of that hospital that's left."

"Do you think that's a bit of a shame? Because there used to be a hospital here for 200 years, a place that I read was just as much a homeless hostel, where people could shower and sleep and eat, and now ... well, there's not; now there are offices and shops. It feels like we could do with more hostels and hospitals for the needy."

There's a pause. I see in his eyes that he realises he's been ambushed, that this "book about land owned by dukes" isn't a boring, historical volume but a savage attack.

"Well ... I suppose ... we, err ... we get involved ... err ... the Duchy has something called the Benevolent Fund ..." — and he waffles a little, lists some charities that he says they support. "I mean ... our funds are limited ... If you read the Duchy financial reports, it might seem like a lot of money, but in the grand scheme of things, it's not a huge amount."

I thought the Adelphi — a few minutes walk from Duchy HQ — might belong to the Duchy of Lancaster; it's a prestigious building that houses, among others, Spotify and *The Economist*. But when I go inside, the receptionist tells me it's owned by Amancio Ortega — that's the bloke who founded Zara. He's owned the building since 2018. He paid £550 million for it.

I circle the Adelphi, thinking maybe the Duchy owned it in the past, and there might be some Duchy insignia carved on its walls or a leftover "DUCHY OF LANCASTER" plaque, but there's not. I do, though, find something interesting: Behind the building, just ten metres from its rear doors, I see a pissy-smelling camp-site ... A row of tents, almost a dozen: a red one, a yellow one, a blue-and-grey one with a tacky tourist plaque stuck on it: "BUCKINGHAM PALACE" ... Some have camping chairs; one's laid out reading a book: *The Great Gatsby*. A shoeless woman chats with a pigeon, and a bloke with an Alsatian devours a bottle of red. As I'm looking at the scene, thinking, *Wow: That's a lot of tents in one place in the capital; there were nights at the campsite I managed that we weren't as busy as this ...* as I'm thinking that, the police come ... "Territorial Support Group" it says on the side of the blue van — a special police unit that deal with "disorder". There are a bunch of officers; some check IDs, some with blue nitrile gloves search the tents ...

A waiter from Smith & Wollensky, an upscale steak-house on the ground floor of the Adelphi, pops out for a fag; he wears a white shirt and a green waistcoat; he speaks with a Spanish accent. "How long have these tents been here?" I ask him.

"So long, actually, that I can't even really remember; two months, at least."

"Is that not a problem for the restaurant and everyone else in the Adelphi?"

"It's a massive problem. Sometimes they're very, very rude, yelling at people walking by, even ladies."

I walk over to the police, and I say, "I'm writing a book about wild camping in the countryside, and I saw this here, and I'm wondering what your policy about this is, about people setting up tents in the middle of London? You'll move them on today?"

"We won't, no."

"Because it's not a criminal offence, right?"

"Right. We're not here now because they're camping here, because of the tents; we're here to investigate possible offences related to drugs."

"Are there many encampments like this around London?"

"Quite a few, yeah."

"And the police never move them on?"

"Not unless there's a criminal offence, no. Tents are for the council to deal with."

Less than a mile from the Savoy Estate, a walk through Leicester Square and Piccadilly Circus — where a tramp in a black parka is comatose on the steps of the famous fountain, hugging a toppled orange traffic cone; where, outside the Criterion Theatre, is a tent structure fashioned from seven umbrellas ("I'm not camping, actually, Mr Council Man, I just really don't like rain.") — a walk through there is Regent Street, adorned with hundreds of Pride flags, where a police car screams past, blue lights flashing, siren wailing, and a Barbiefied double-decker passes, it's red now pink to advertise the movie out this week; and I walk along there and down Vigo Street into Mayfair, to Savile Row ... and here, at No.1 Savile Row, is Gieves & Hawkes, where a large Union Jack hangs over the pillared entrance of the ritzy, white building where Charles's £5,000 double-breasted, wide-lapelled, navy blue suits are tailored. A three-minute walk from Savile Row is Grosvenor Street, where Swiss watches retail for tens of thousands, and a store called Princess advertises bespoke yachts. Grosvenor Street leads to Grosvenor Square, the country's second-priciest locale ...

The park here — a calm, green refuge; benches, shady trees — like Russell Square was "PRIVATE" until WWII when its iron railings were pulled down for the war. A sign at the entrance says, "... In 1946, through the generosity of the 2nd Duke of Westminster, the garden became a public space for everyone's enjoyment ..." *Generosity?* Hmm ... The freehold is still with the Grosvenors — the freehold for this land that, remember, was acquired when a Grosvenor ancestor married 12-year-old Mary Davies. Along the square's west side is what was the US Embassy; it's now being morphed by Qatari Diar into a five-star hotel — The Chancery Rosewood — but a large golden eagle still sits atop it. The US wanted to buy that land but were told they couldn't; the Grosvenors said they would, in line with their standard policy, only lease it — no exceptions for a country that helped Britain defeat the Nazis. The Grosvenors, incidentally, owned lots of land in the US before the American Revolution; when the US won the War of Independence, the Grosvenor's US lands were confiscated. Duke Street runs from Grosvenor Square to Oxford Street, which is the northern boundary of Mayfair. I see in the window of an estate agent a listing for Duke Street: to rent a three-bedroom apartment, £27,733 a month. Past Grosvenor House, I turn onto Aldford Street, and at the end of that street is Grosvenor Chapel: A blue door, a spire with a clock, a portico over the pavement ... A man is asleep under the portico, on a cardboard mattress, wrapped up in a sleeping bag like a mouldy burrito.

Park Lane is the west margin of Mayfair, and at Hyde Park Corner, where Park Lane meets Piccadilly — Mayfair's southern border — is a grand, yellowy aristocratic building, fronted by pillars; this is Apsley House: the London residence of the Duke of Wellington. In this area too: Wellington Arch, a couple of Wellington statues, a road named Duke of Wellington Place ... The 1st Duke of Wellington purchased this house, so no complaints about that. *This* house wasn't handed to him, but, in 1817, he was gifted another house and a block of land with it; those 7,000 acres — 4,000 football pitches — are in Hampshire, and those acres are "PRIVATE". You and I can access 350 of those acres — Wellington Country Park — if we pay £18.95 and leave by 17:30; to camp there, it's £45 a night — a two-night minimum stay. We're now on our 9th Duke of Wellington. No one would seriously quarrel with the 1st Duke having that land — he master-minded Napoleon's defeat — but this runt now, 200 years later? What's *he* done for it? Sure, gift land to people who put the great in Great Britain. Why not? All kinds of candidates for that: Winston Churchill, Florence Nightingale, Emmeline Pankhurst, David Attenborough, Hermione Granger, Bobby Moore ... Yes, give them some acres as a thanks. But not *forever*. Attenborough might be cool, but his son or his grandson ... or his great-great-great-great-great-great-great grandson, might be a narcissistic, fascist arse — or, at least, a vanilla-flavoured nothingburger. Give them the acres while they're alive, then take them back when they're dead and give them to someone else great; give them to Attenborough until he dies, then hand those acres to, say, Liam Gallagher. (Or, maybe, don't dish out any land; a road, an arch, a couple of statues, a countryside mansion ... might be thanks enough.)

I walk away from Wellington Arch and straight onto a street that runs off it: Grosvenor Crescent — the 4th most expensive street in the UK. On a red telephone box at the start of the street, someone's plastered stickers: "BRAZILIAN BABE! (0)(0) 07709360139" ... "BARBIE DOLL XXX 07051 ..." It's a curved street of white, graceful 19th-century houses with delightful flowering window boxes; above the door to No.17 are the black, yellow, and red stripes of Belgium — their embassy. Where Grosvenor Crescent meets Belgrave Square is a statue of a lordly man in a cloak with his foot on a milestone: "Chester: 197 Miles". The Grosvenor coat of arms is on the base of the statue, along with a quote: "When we build, let us think we build forever." There's a map, too, which shows their Belgravia empire; they own 300 acres of Belgravia, which is nearly the same size as Hyde Park: 350 acres.

Fifty-or-so elegant houses bound Belgrave Square, some of which are embassies — Germany, Turkey, Serbia ... There's a park in the middle of the square that's the size of 2.5 football pitches. In one corner is a statue of Simon Bolivar; in another, a statue of Jose de San Martin: two *Libertadores* — Latin Americans who led the revolutions that seized their land back from the Spanish. The park is "PRIVATE". It's so "PRIVATE" that they're even picky about what dogs go in: a sign says, "All Dogs Must Be Registered With Grosvenor." I'll go in: Just a stroll and a chill, not a dirty protest in the children's playground or scissoring the tennis court net. Hedges on the inner side of the railings make it hard to get in for most of the way around, but to leap one of the four gates is easy. I leap the gate opposite the Embassy of Bahrain ...

It's more woody than Bedford Square or Grosvenor Square — a very scenic space. I stroll the paths, see lush trees, rose bushes, wisteria-covered pergolas, Doric-columned shelters ... There's a sundial in the shape of a globe, and there's a statue called *Homage to Vitruvian Man*, sculpted by Enzo Plazzotta; which sounds fancy but is just a statue of a bloke with his dick out. A posh man walks by me, on the phone: "... I'm not moving to Brussels unless they offer me a *huge* sum of money to do so ..." The only other people I see are a guy jogging the outer path and a woman walking a designer doggie. No one questions me about being here, and why would they? I'm just a quiet fella on a bench, reading *The Times* ...

"Duke 'Dined With Epstein During His House Arrest':
The Duke of York visited Jeffrey Epstein while the

paedophile financier was under house arrest for sex
offences, new court documents suggest ..."

Off Belgrave Square is a street named Belgrave Place,
and I walk down there, past Belgrave Mews and Eaton
Place and Eccleston Mews, to Eaton Square ... The grand
houses here have pillared porches and black doors with
lion heads for door-knockers, and there are six more
~~gardens~~ parks: paths and lawns and trees. Signs at each
say, "... These gardens are the property of the Grosvenor
Estate ... Under no circumstances should garden entry fobs
be loaned to any person ..." No hedges beside the railings
here, so it's easy to climb in anywhere, not just at the gates.
They're all empty — six leafy oases in chaotic, cramped
London and *no one* in any of them.

I walk Upper Belgrave Street, past a big, blue Rolls-
Royce, and come to Chester Street — very quiet, very
swanky; a black Bentley with the number plate MI6 TOP
— and that leads to Grosvenor Place, a road that's lined on
one side by a wall ... The wall looks like that of a prison: a
high brick wall, barbed wire, sharp spikes, cameras. The
wall circles Buckingham Palace and "the largest private
garden in the capital". I won't climb *this* wall. Sod that. In
these times of suicide bombers, men with backpacks
scaling *this* wall are shot. In the past, in an age more innocent, it was easier ... It was very easy for Michael Fagan on
July 9th 1982: At 06:45 that day, he scaled this wall and
walked through the grounds to Buckingham Palace, and
shinnied up a drainpipe and entered through an unlocked
window. He wandered around barefoot and, after nosing at
George V's stamp collection, found the Queen's bedroom.
Elizabeth was in there, in her nightie in her four-poster
bed. She rang an alarm, but no one came, so she ushered

babbling Fagan out of the room by telling him she had some cigarettes in the pantry. He ended up arrested but never went to jail, as he hadn't threatened, hadn't damaged, hadn't stolen. When asked why he did it, Fagan said he'd had a large dose of magic mushrooms. He later recorded a version of *God Save The Queen* with a band called the Bollock Brothers.

Grosvenor Place runs onto Lower Grosvenor Place, which leads onto Buckingham Palace Road, which becomes Buckingham Gate; and above 10 Buckingham Gate flies a flag: black with a yellow inverted triangle: the flag of the Duke of Cornwall. This is the headquarters of the Duchy of Cornwall, where William works from 09:00 to 17:00 to earn his £24 million a year; he commutes here — fifteen minutes in an Uber — from Kensington Palace, where he lives ... No, of course not: He's rarely in that house, seldom in this office. He lives on the royal estate at Windsor — which Aaron Barschak turned up at in 2003 to gatecrash William's 21st birthday party ...

Aaron was dressed as Osama bin Laden in drag — a peach ball gown. He climbed some walls and gates, strolled around a while, then burst onto a stage where William — wearing a loincloth — was giving a speech to a crowd that included Charles — dressed as a tribal chief – and the Queen, who was wearing a purple Swazi outfit. (It was an African-themed party.) Aaron snatched the microphone from William and spent a minute performing a comedy routine, then kissed William on the cheek and went to the bar to get some champagne. At this point, someone questioned who the hell he was and if he should be there. He was arrested, initially under terrorism laws, but all charges were dropped because, the police said, he hadn't committed an offence. He was on stage at Windsor

Castle at William's 21st birthday party, performing unre-
quested stand-up in front of the Queen, and doing that
while dressed as a transvestite Osama bin Laden, and that
— *even that* — wasn't enough for aggravated trespass.

That stunt led to calls to make ordinary trespass on
royal estates — estates where royalty reside, *not* the Duchy
estates — a criminal offence, and there are now signs on
the walls around Buckingham Palace Garden: "This is a
protected site under section 128 of the Serious Organised
Crime and Police Act 2005. Trespass on this site is a criminal offence." That, unlike typical trespass signs, isn't bullshit. So you now can't trespass at Buckingham Palace, St
James's Palace, Kensington Palace, Highgrove House,
Sandringham House, or Windsor Castle, but the rest of
Duchyland remains open — like, for example, Syon
House, the Duke of Northumberland's mansion in
London, which is where I'm going now ...

I take the Underground to Boston Manor, and I walk
down Boston Manor Road to the centre of Brentford, past
squat, squeezed terraces with Ford-Fiesta-sized yards.
Overhead, the constant growl of 737s as they fly over on
their descent to Heathrow. Ravers stream along the road
with me, en route to Junction 2 at Boston Manor Park,
where Adam Beyer and Jeff Mills are on the bill. As I pass
the park, hear the thumping techno bang out, I'm tempted,
very goddamn tempted, by a chemical-induced knees-up,
but I don't want to turn up at Ralph's — that's his name,
the 12th Duke of Northumberland, the man 286th on *The
Sunday Times* Rich List 2023 (£500 million) — I don't want
to turn up at his house sweaty and twisted and gurning. If
the 11th duke were still the boss, to turn up off my face
would have been fine, and, indeed, we might have been
great friends, but the 11th duke — Ralph's older brother —

was in 1995 found dead by his valet, slumped beside his bed at Syon House ... Heart failure, a result of guzzling amphetamines.

I walk along Brentford High Street, past Greggs and MiMi Nails & Hair, and I turn down Half Moon Close and walk a lane to a big, black gate; on the gate is a large blue sign with a gold lion on it: "SYON — THE LONDON HOME OF THE DUKE OF NORTHUMBERLAND". The gate is open, and I continue along the lane beside a brick wall, a few metres tall ... and as I come out of the lane and see the stately mansion, fronted by a couple of turrets, I see too a sign on the wall that says, "Syon House takes its name from Syon Abbey, which stood on the site now occupied by Syon House .... The abbey was suppressed in 1539 by Henry VIII ... The estate was gifted to Henry Percy, the 9th Earl of Northumberland, in 1604, and has remained in the family's ownership to the present day." That's not Henry VIII's only link to this house: When the twat at last died in 1547, his body spent a night here on its journey to Windsor; his fat corpse, gassy and rotting after hanging around in London for a week, literally exploded. Before anyone realised, hounds had chewed pieces of Henry.

I'm not actually trespassing *at the moment*, as I'm on a public footpath; the path runs from the gate I entered through to the other side of the estate. *Great!* But, percentage-wise, the car park here takes up more space than the slender footpath. Less than 1% of this estate is open for free. £9 it costs to enter the garden behind the wall. It's closed now. It's open from 10:30 to 16:30 for half of the year; it's closed completely from October to March. You can also pay for a look inside Ralph's home, but "home" is misleading as he doesn't reside here. His wife told the *Financial Times*, "In winter, the family lives at Alnwick

Castle, and in summer, we're in the Scottish Borders." Ralph's winter residence, Alnwick Castle, starred as Hogwarts in *The Philosopher's Stone* and *The Chamber of Secrets*. It was at that castle that Potter learnt Quidditch, and there that Ron crash-landed the Weasley family's flying car into the Whomping Willow. Harry and Ron would go there on the Hogwarts Express from King's Cross Station to Hogsmeade Station — the real station at Goathland was used for that, which is on the Duchy of Lancaster's Yorkshire estate (10,000 acres).

This estate here is 200 acres, which is a crumb compared to the Percy's northern kingdom ... Ralph has 100,000 acres up there — 57,000 football pitches. In England, only the Duchy of Cornwall is larger than Ralph's empire. How did the Percys get so much land? Their ancestor, William de Percy, was a buddie of William the Conqueror ... The Northumberland Estates website says, "The Percys are mentioned in the *Domesday Book* as owning 118 manors in Lincolnshire, Yorkshire, Essex ..." That book, incidentally — that very book, the original — is kept 3 km from here at The National Archives, on the other side of the Thames, beside Kew Gardens. Next to Kew Gardens, directly over the river from Syon House, is the 300-acre Royal Mid-Surrey Golf Club — two 18-hole courses — which is on land owned by the Crown Estate: 300 acres of juicy green in London that could be for the people but is instead "PRIVATE" — and Charles banking 25% of the rent for it via the Sovereign Grant.

Most of Ralphistan is "PRIVATE", but bits and pieces are open, like, for example, Hulne Park near the centre of Alnwick: 3,000 acres within a walled enclosure — "once the hunting grounds of the Percy family". It's open to the public — not dogs, though, even on a lead; and bicycles aren't allowed — but you have to "stick to the marked routes", and, says their website, it's open only "from 11:00 until 16:00 each day, when the gates are closed". Which means for people — the majority — who have to work 09:00 to 17:00, those 3,000 acres are only accessible on Saturday and Sunday — 10 hours a week. Alnwick, by the way, is just 30 km from the England-Scotland border ... *Scotland*: That strange, foreign country with that odd law that gives people the right to walk where they want.

In *Whose Britain Is It Anyway?* — a BBC documentary from 2006 — Ralph is up north in his realm, stood fishing in a forest next to a river — *his* forest, *his* river — and when asked about the benefits of owning a lot of land, he says, "There's a lot of pleasure in it. I'm passionate about fishing, so it's rather nice to be able to pop down whenever I want to and cast a fly, and I love the shooting and everything else that goes with the countryside." There's talk of the agricultural subsidies Ralph receives and how crucial they are for him to be able to hold onto so much land, and then he's asked, "Do you think it's rather anomalous that, in the 21st century, you have all this land and so many other people have so little?"

Ralph says, "It doesn't feel to me as if I own huge tracts of land because I share it with other people, in one form or another."

"But *you're* the owner."

There's an awkward silence. "I'm the owner, I suppose."

At the end of that show, they said what I've stated already about the size of the land hoarded by the aristocracy: that it's at least 25% of the country ... Imagine, for example, playing Monopoly against someone who starts with 25% of the squares on the board as theirs ... Hardly fair, is it?

But, fair or not, as it stands, Ralph is, I suppose, the owner of this land I'm on, and as the owner, I suppose he gets to make the rules, and one of his rules, I suppose, is no camping. No signs here say "NO CAMPING", and they didn't reply to my email — "I accept my invitation to visit you ..." — to say that I couldn't camp, but, I suppose, that's one of Ralph's rules.

Ralph would prefer I stump up for the 137-room Syon Hilton that's on the estate: £150 a night. Where the hotel is, there used to be the London Butterfly House — three large greenhouses; thousands of butterflies from around the world, as well as birds and reptiles and insects; the only attraction of its kind in the city — but that was bulldozed by Ralph in 2007 to build this hotel. These dukes, the aristocracy, they're "guardians" or "custodians" of the countryside and it's "preservation" and "conservation" ... until they can earn a buck from that land. Then it's golf courses, retail parks, Hiltons, mines ... The Percys, as their website admits, garnered "immense wealth" from coal.

I'm not paying for the Hilton ...

That high brick wall is between the footpath and the garden; no way I can climb that. But I don't need to because only half the estate is behind that wall; the other half is spread before me ... And it's very, very nice; as their website says, it "feels like deep countryside, although barely nine miles from Charing Cross". Hyde Park is seven miles from here; Hyde Park that was, like here, one of Henry VIII's seizures in the dissolution of the monasteries ... Hyde Park was "PRIVATE" for a while and then opened to the peasants. Regent's Park too — near Bloomsbury — those 410 acres were seized in the 1500s but later turned from "PRIVATE" to public. But not here, not Ralph's land. So people in Brentford have to make do with Boston

Manor Park, a mile from here. It's 34 acres, much smaller than this estate; plus, the M4 cuts through Boston Manor Park — yes, an effing motorway.

Across Park Road from the path is an open meadow: long grass and wildflowers and bushy trees and two dozen cows. It's "PRIVATE", and on the low, feeble fence that blocks off that meadow are yellow triangle warning signs: "BULL IN FIELD". Screw them and their bull: *If* there's a bull in this meadow — and there very well may not be, as I can't see one, and it's the sort of sign they'd put up to keep people out of this meadow, whether there's a bull in it or not — but even *if* there is, it's not a wild animal that happens to have chosen this spot. It's Ralph's damn bull, and he chose to put it in this meadow, chose to cordon off a chunk of prime loveliness in London for the sake of a bull, a bull that he could have put somewhere else — like, for instance, on the other side of his big wall. It's the same scam as the "DEER RESERVE": "Sorry, we'd love to let you go on that land, but we can't because of the bull."

I cross the meadow, spring over a little fence, and come to a long lake; a few swans in it, an ornate bridge over it, some trees scattered around it. I walk beside the water to a woody area at the end of it ... a fine spot to camp. No security from what I've seen, but, anyway, if they do stumble upon me — and I doubt it, as I'm far from any road, and it's past 21:00 — but if they do see me and kick up a fuss, I'll tell them to lodge a complaint with the council.

ROYAL COURTS OF JUSTICE

A woman shouts: "When *I* say who's moor, *you* say our moor ... Who's moor?"

The crowd (me too) yell: "OUR MOOR!"

"Who's moor?"

"OUR MOOR!"

"When *I* say right, *you* say to roam ... Right!"

"TO ROAM!"

"Right!"

"TO ROAM!"

I said I'd never stand in the street and yell, that I wouldn't be one of *those* people, but ... well ... here I am, on the Strand, standing in front of a grey, gothic building, all arches and spires and pomp — the Royal Courts of Justice — stood beside someone who appears to have woken up in a swamp, and I'm yelling ... I even have a placard: "The Spirit Of Dartmoor! Old Crockern Rises!" Other placards state: "Nature Is A Human Right!", "Moor Camping, Not Less Right To Roam!", "Camping IS Recreation, Obviously!" ... There's a white banner, "RIGHT TO ROAM", and a black banner, "THE STARS ARE FOR EVERYONE". There's a woman in a wheelchair with a flute and rainbow shoelaces, and a shaved-headed woman with a whistle — she orchestrates the drummers banging tribal beats. The merry pagan troupe from Dartmoor in January are also here — green-splashed faces, brown, baggy trousers, flowery crowns; skipping and dancing and whooping, clapping wooden sticks as one of them croons into a megaphone. Old Crockern *isn't* here ... London can't handle *that*.

I just came to watch, but then I got caught up in the affair; those tribal beats sort of seeped into my brain, and when a woman handing out placards asked if I wanted one, I thought: Yeah, why not? And once I had a placard, I couldn't not chant, could I? Still ... I'm here with them, but I'm not affiliated with them; be clear on that, as I'm sure that after some of the nonsense I've vomited on these pages, they'd prefer to distance me from their *respectable* campaign for improved access to land. But to the passers-by, to the faces peering out from the shiny black cabs, to the tourists on the open-topped buses staring down at us — the Saudis and Indians and Chinese snapping this circus — to them, the fact I'm wearing skinny jeans and brown flip-flops and holding a placard with a picture of Old Crockern on it means I'm just like the rest of the hundred or so plebs in this rally. The passers-by and the tourists will lump me in with the rest, and so will the press and all the people who read or watch the news ... The BBC are here, *The Guardian* ... TV cameras and photographers; massive lenses, furry microphones ... My face will be in the news today — my face and my placard.

Lewis, chief of The Stars Are For Everyone, stands on a stone bench in front of the crowd and press: "It started with just a handful of us, five or so, meeting in a pub, down about the possible loss of our cherished wild camping rights on Dartmoor. That was last December, but it wasn't until January that we found out the news that we had, indeed, lost the right to wild camp on Dartmoor, an absolutely devastating blow to all that care about access to land, about people's connection to our landscape. We witnessed the snatching away of a beloved right, and so we stood up against greed and self-servitude. 3,000 people took to Dartmoor in January — the biggest land rights protest in England in decades — and now, here we are, this July, outside the Royal Courts of Justice, while the appeal is heard inside ..."

Inside, the appeal is in the hands of three judges: Vos, Newey, and Underhill; and we, out here, know exactly what's being discussed in there, in Court No.71, because Court No.71 is being live-streamed on YouTube ...

The case hinges on the definition of "open-air recreation", the term used in section 10 of the Dartmoor Commons Act 1985, which is the legislation that, until January this year, gave people the right to wild camp on Dartmoor — people having the right to access Dartmoor "for the purpose of open-air recreation". The judge for the case in January ruled that wild camping didn't count as open-air recreation, which is why the legal right to do so on Dartmoor disappeared. The Dartmoor National Park Authority (DNPA) brought an appeal, which is being heard right now, and Straker, the lawyer for the DNPA, is arguing that, surely, sleeping overnight on Dartmoor so you can marvel at the sunset in a wild, wide-open landscape, and, in darkness and silence, blissfully survey the stars, away from the clutter of modernity, and wake in the morning to a magical sunrise over ancient tors, serenaded by a chorus of birds, surely, Straker says, that *is* recreation. Morshead, the lawyer for Dickwart, is saying, no, that's bollocks; he's saying wild camping is essentially sleeping, and sleeping *isn't* recreation because you're asleep; he's saying a critical component of recreation is enjoyment, and it's not possible to enjoy sleep. Morshead is quizzed about a hypothetical person who takes a nap in the day: If someone is on a long hike and lays down for a half-hour snooze, should that person then be booted off the moor? Does it depend on whether the snooze was pre-planned or spontaneous? And if snoozing is permitted, at what point does the snooze become sleep? One hour? Three hours? And how could that be policed? Rangers with stopwatches running around Dartmoor timing how long someone's eyes have been closed? And what are those rangers to do about a person sleepwalking? Or what if a person is inside a tent, but they're not asleep — is that allowed? And what to do about other types of temporary structures that might be used for recreation: How about pop-up inflatable goalposts for children to have a kickabout — is that acceptable?

The Dartmoor Preservation Association crowdfunded £60,000 of donations for the appeal's legal costs, and one of their guys, Tom, gets up on the stone bench — "... The initial judgement was a further assault, in a long series of assaults, on rights we have to access nature, which is why this appeal is so critical to this entire movement ..." — then up steps a woman called Mary-Ann, an archaeologist who was once a model for Kellogg's Special K: "I want to talk to you about my first experience wild camping ... I was 27, and I said to my friend Hannah, I said, 'I'm going camping on Dartmoor,' and she said, 'But where are you actually going to sleep?', and I said, 'A flat bit that isn't a bog.' She said,

'But where will you go to the toilet?' I said, 'I've got a trow-el.' She paused, then she said, 'You'll be murdered!' And that, more or less, was a conversation I had multiple times in the week before I first went to Dartmoor. I was telling people what I was doing, hoping they would gee me up, yet every single one of them told me I was going to be murdered ... Anyway, I got an army-surplus tent off eBay, and I got on the bus and then the train, and I then walked onto the wild moor, and my head was exploding with excitement and terror — terror because Dartmoor, I'd been led to believe, is where murderers live, not in, say, London. Out on the moor, the weather was glorious, and I was thrilled — thrilled with the sense of freedom. I wasn't going to a campsite where there would be other people and where there would be Andrex in the toilets. I was on an adventure — *on my own*. It was just the land and me, and that was, I admit, a little scary, but that's where the growth comes from, isn't it? ... Since that first time, that liberating experience at Dartmoor, I've taken other people wild camping at other places, and the question that's always asked is, 'Are we allowed to do this?' And the answer is, 'No, not really, but it will probably be alright, as no one will see us do it.' For some people, that answer is a thrill, but for other people, not so much; and I include myself in that — I'm someone who at a train station will only walk up and down the stairs where the arrows tell me I can do. I don't like breaking rules. But I do wild camp, even though it's not allowed, because I don't think there should be a rule about where I can wild camp responsibly and sustainably and discreetly. I don't, though, take my young child wild camping, even though I want to, because if I were to set up our tent in time to make him his tea on our stove and get him ready for bedtime, I worry that we would be too conspicuous, that we would be challenged and asked to move on, and I fear that then my child's memory of that day wouldn't be one of freedom and quiet joy under the stars, but that their memory of that day would be the time that mummy got told off by that stranger."

The MC says, "Next up, one of Right to Roam's most ardent supporters and allies, right from the very beginning leading debate on nature access in parliament ... Please put your hands together for Green Party MP, and twice leader of that party, Caroline Lucas!"

The crowd: "WOOOOOOO!!!"

"It's wonderful to be with you here today to stand up against those who seek to cut us off from the land that we call home. We should, really, thank this hedge fund manager for inadvertently galvanising a movement that will lead to the biggest shake-up of land rights in a generation!"

The crowd: "WOOOOOOO!!!"

"Some may claim we can't be trusted to walk or to camp in our green and pleasant landscape, but we know that isn't true; we know that it's not us, not the public, that is the threat to nature. To borrow some words from Right to Roam campaigner Nick Hayes, 'It's not the wild swimmer that poisons our rivers, nor the rambler that burns the moorlands.' ... We will not accept that, in England, we have legal access to just 8% of rural land, while our friends north of the border have the freedom to walk, to camp, almost anywhere, provided they exercise that freedom responsibly. We will not be denied the right to explore our woodlands, marvelling at the bluebells and listening to the birdsong. We will not be denied the right to bathe in our lakes and to swim in our rivers. We will not be denied the right to sleep under the night sky, as humans have done for millennia. And we will not be denied the right to know, and to love, and to protect our beautiful and infinitely precious isle ... I believe the time has come to put an end to the exclusion that cuts us off from the beauty all around us, and I believe we *will* see a new Right to Roam Act that recognises we're not separate from nature but deeply part of it!"

The crowd: "WOOOOOOO!!!"

The MC says, "And now our last speaker, Guy Shrubsole!"

The crowd: "WOOOOOOO!!!"

Supreme Leader Shrubsole steps up onto the bench ... "On that January day, when thousands of us gathered on the slopes of Dartmoor, we made history, and I'll never forget the sight of that great sea of people stretching out over the moor, the beating of drums and the fluttering banners, and the roar of voices when Old Crockern appeared. That day was when I thought: We've won already, regardless of any defeats ahead of us. We may lose today's appeal, but I know that, even if we do, we won't lose for long because the great tidal wave that has been unleashed can't be held back. Since that winter day on the moor, the campaign's momentum only increases. The very next week, the Labour Party announced it would, if it's elected to government, support a Right to Roam Act for England; and, a few months later, in a parliamentary debate organised by Caroline Lucas, a Labour spokesperson declared they'd adopt the system of access rights used now in Scotland, where, for the last 20 years, people have enjoyed full rights of responsible access to nearly all land and water, through the Land Reform Act that was passed in 2003 ..."

Scotland: What exactly is going on in that far-off, weird country? There's a website (https://www.outdooraccess-scotland.scot) with a comprehensive 130-page PDF, which covers every what-if imaginable, but it's an extremely boring read, so I'll save you the hassle of having to pore through the whole thing by giving you the meat of it ...

Scottish Outdoor Access Code
Public Access To Scotland's Outdoors: Your Rights And Responsibilities

"The Land Reform Act 2003 gives everyone statutory access rights to most land and inland water, at any time of day or night, providing they exercise those rights responsibly. You can exercise these access rights in places such as:

— Hills, mountains, and moorland;

— Woods and forests;

— Rivers, canals, and reservoirs;

— Beaches and the coastline;

— Land in which crops have not been sown;

— On the margins of fields where crops are growing or have been sown;

— Fields where there are horses, cattle, and other farm animals;

— Golf courses, but only for crossing them and providing that you don't take access across greens or interfere with any games of golf."

"You can exercise access rights for recreational purposes, which includes:

— Pastimes, such as watching wildlife, sightseeing, painting, and photography;

— Family and social activities, such as picnics, playing, sledging, paddling, or flying a kite;

— Active pursuits, such as cycling, horse riding, rock climbing, canoeing, swimming, windsurfing, sailing, and wild camping."

Access rights don't apply to a range of places, like school fields, visitor attractions with paid entry, building sites, airfields ... and people's gardens:

"The Land Reform Act 2003 states that you can't exercise access rights on 'sufficient adjacent land' next to a house. For most houses, this should be reasonably obvious: a formal garden next to the house and surrounded by a wall, hedge, or fence. In some cases, the garden might be more difficult to identify, perhaps because there's no obvious boundary such as a wall, fence, or hedge; in that case, things to look out for in judging whether an area of land close to a house is a garden or not include: a lawn or other area of short mown grass; flowerbeds and tended shrubs, paving, and water features. Some larger houses are surrounded by quite large areas of land. These are usually areas of grassland, parkland, or woodland. Here, too, you will need to make a judgement in the light of the particular circumstances. Parts may be intensively managed for the domestic enjoyment of the house and include lawns, flowerbeds, paths, seats, sheds, water features, and summerhouses. Access rights don't extend to these intensively managed areas. The wider, less intensively managed parts, such as grassland and woodlands, whether enclosed or not, aren't classed as a garden, and so access rights can be exercised."

The Land Reform Act 2003 and the Scottish Outdoor Access Code don't offer a free-for-all for criminal activity on private land: If a person litters when on that land, it's still an offence under the Environmental Protection Act 1990; if someone doesn't clean up their dog's mess when they're on that land, they can be charged by virtue of the Dog Fouling Act 2003; if, while on that land, a bloke buggers an unwilling protected species, he'll be in court for breaching the Wildlife & Countryside Act 1981 ... Even aggravated trespass is still an offence in Scotland; if, while on private land, a person does anything to obstruct or disrupt lawful activity on that land, then the Criminal Justice and Public Order Act 1994 still applies.

Clear and sensible, right?

And it's worked in Scotland for 20 years ... It's worked in Scotland on Dickwart's 16,000-acre estate there — yes, his 4,000 acres in Dartmoor aren't all he owns. It's worked in Scotland on the Duke of Buccleuch's 61,000-acre estate near Selkirk, which is less than 100 km from the Duke of Northumberland's northern estate. It's a massive anomaly in Britain that to roam and camp on the Duke of Buccleuch's Scottish estate is fine, but it's not fine 90 minutes drive away, on the Duke of Northumberland's English estate; nor on the Duke of Buccleuch's English estate — 11,000 acres near Kettering in Northamptonshire — which is "PRIVATE".

The typical argument against is "... parties ... littering ... scorched patches of grass ..." And, yes, that happens *some-times*, as evidenced by the "wild camping" freak-out photos that pop up now and then in *Farmers Weekly* and the *Daily Mail* — "Look what they've done! The filthy swine, the goddamn townies!" Those photos, there are always beer cans all over the floor, and often broken camping chairs and frisbees and disposable barbecues and laughing gas canisters and packets of Doritos and spliff ends ... But that's not wild campers, not really. No wild camper carries a frisbee and a camping chair and a case of 24 Carling with them on a hike — to keep the weight of my bag down, I now don't even pack an airbed. What those photos show is not a mess that wild campers made but the foul aftermath of dumbasses partying. I've been a partying dumbass enough to know. In our drunken jackass years, friends and I made plenty of messes exactly like those in each other's gardens. "Wild camping" bomb sites aren't a wild camping problem but a drinking problem; in the same way that drink-driving accidents aren't a driving issue but a drink one. The severe penalty for that is mostly a sufficient deterrent: almost no one drinks and drives, even though the chances of being caught are small. It's just not worth the risk. If the punishment for countryside partying was harsh — months in prison, thousands of pounds as a fine — who would bother to risk it?

It's lame to make laws that affect everyone based on a very, very small percentage misbehaving. We shouldn't let that 0.1% dictate the law for the 99.9% ... To say *no one* can roam or wild camp because *some* people will litter is like saying *no one* can ride a bicycle because *some* people cycle on the pavement. It's like saying that because *some* people don't clear up their dog's mess from the street or park, *no one* can walk their dog. You can apply that odd logic to literally goddamn everything: letting *no one* do something because *some* people are tossers when they do that thing. But that odd logic isn't applied to everything; it's applied to almost nothing. But, for some reason, it's applied to the right to roam and wild camping — in England, anyway, but not in Scotland.

They, in Scotland, have full rights of responsible access to nearly all land; we, in England, are so far behind that we no longer even have the right, by law, to wild camp on Dartmoor — the last 0.2% of England where people could.

And that won't change today: We won't know the verdict of the appeal for weeks.

DOWN SOUTH

This is the second strangest place I've slept. The strangest was Bloomfield Road, where, one November morning long ago, when I was 19, and drunk friends and I had been booted out of a B&B at silly o'clock for being rowdy, I woke up fully clothed in Blackpool's football stadium — fully clothed except for my socks, which, for some reason I'll never know, were in my pockets. Today, I haven't woken up somewhere quite as odd as that, but still, it's odd: a golf course on the Duke of Richmond's Goodwood Estate.

Last night, I pitched my tent in the woods near the tee-off spot for Hole 9 (par 4, 427 yards). The duke — Charles — *might* not mind, as he told the *Evening Standard* that it's not "like a normal golf club, which can be very stuffy". He also told them, "People can play in jeans and flip-flops — I don't mind." And on the "Values" page of his website, one of his core values is "Derring-Do" — "We don't mind breaking the rules to create the best possible experiences ..." Another value is "The Real Thing — Authenticity" — "... experiences as they should be, resulting in pure, unspoiled, unadulterated pleasure."

Wild camping is "breaking the rules", and it's camping as it should be, pure and unspoiled, and I'm wearing jeans and flip-flops ... So, yeah, he *might* not mind. (He didn't reply to my email telling him I was coming, so I can't be sure.)

I yesterday walked here from Chichester, which is a few miles away. Not a long walk but not a fun one, as I had to scurry along roadside slivers of grass verge like a fox as cars whipped past me; I was, many times, pinned in thorny hedges to dodge trucks. I passed Goodwood Aerodrome and Goodwood Motor Circuit. I saw hangars and grandstands, heard big engines thrumming around the track; dinky planes buzzed around overhead. I passed a massive, grassy field with a sign: "Car Park C". A security guard was at the entrance to that car park, sitting on a camping chair; a pleb paid £10.42 an hour (which I know because I looked at the job listings on the estate website). He's paid £10.42 an hour — minimum wage — by a duke worth over £200 million.

Sick of slow progress dangerously tramping along the road, I climbed a fence into one of the duke's fields to walk there instead. That field was Car Park A, and that field was humungous — that field and the field for Car Park C are larger than any of Chichester's public parks. Car Park A was empty when I walked across it, but when it's full, it can house thousands of cars; I know that because on Google Earth I saw it packed with thousands of cars. Google Earth showed other fields jam-packed with campers. You can camp on this estate *sometimes*. You can camp for one of their marquee motorsport events: Goodwood Revival or the Festival of Speed ... The Festival of Speed is every July, and 200,000 people swamp the estate for that. To camp here then costs about £300 —

which is on top of the ticket for the event, which is over £200.

I came out of Car Park A and walked along a road to the £210-a-night Goodwood Hotel, which had a little path at its side that came onto a drive lined with cedar trees. A white pick-up truck branded with the Goodwood emblem — a crown, lions, etc. — drove past me but didn't stop to ask what I was up to; for all he knew, I was a hotel guest ... In the hotel section of their website, it says: "Exclusive access is given to our hotel guests to walk through the historic park and ancient woodland around the 11,000-acre Goodwood Estate." If asked, I'd have said, "Room 213. Doctor Thompson," and I doubt they would have checked. At a bend of the drive, which carried on up to Goodwood House — where Charles lives — I turned off it and threaded between some greens and bunkers to these woods, and here I slept. It wasn't a great night's kip, as I was too darn hot — the sleeping bag that kept me warm in April boiled me in August. Sleeping naked would have helped — how I'd normally sleep in bed — but I stay clothed when I sleep on these camping ventures because I know that if I'm somehow arrested and charged, in court, I'll be labelled a "naked wild camper" ... By the time it reaches the tabloids: "NUDE PERVERT Caught ILLE-GALLY Camping!!!"

Golf here starts at 07:30, so I pack up before that and walk back onto the drive, which is marked with rubber skids from racers' tyres. During the Festival of Speed, F1 cars zoom along here, and there's rally racing at nearby woodland: Birdless Grove. I pass near the Big House — a strange-shaped building (three sides of an octagon) with an ivy-covered facade and four circular towers topped by domes. I'm so close, I can almost see through the duke's windows, and I could, if I wanted, go up to the fancy-columned entrance and knock on his door, as there are no gates in front of the house. But if I knock on his door, what will I say? Nothing worthwhile, no doubt, and the risk of saying nothing worthwhile is a punch in the face ... Because this duke is right to be a little jumpy about random strangers on his doorstep after he was viciously burgled in 2016: He was bashed unconscious at 04.30 by a ski-masked burglar who'd scaled a ladder and entered an upstairs window. His wife was tied up. The thieving weasel made off with £700,000 of jewellery, including an emerald ring that Charles II gifted his French mistress, Louise de Kerouaille — their bastard child, Charles Lennox, became the 1st Duke of Richmond in 1675, when he was three years old.

A vast, grassy expanse sprinkled with clusters of trees is in front of the Big House — "picturesque parkland" is how the duke's website describes it. I stroll over it, past a cricket pitch with a thatch-roofed pavilion, and enter Seeley Copse on New Barn Hill ... This is the spot for one of the activities available for guests at the hotel. "Forest Bathing", they call it: "Escape into the heart of the forest at Good-wood for your own mindfulness treatment." They provide a link to the website of the National Trust for more information ...

"Forest bathing or '*shinrin-yoku*' was first developed in Japan in the 1980s, following scientific studies conducted by the government. The results showed that two hours of mindful exploration in a forest could reduce blood pressure, lower levels of the stress hormone cortisol, and improve concentration and memory. They also found that trees release chemicals called phytoncides, which have a protective antimicrobial effect on human bodies and thereby boost the immune system. As a result of this research, the Japanese government introduced *'shinrin-yoku'* as a national health programme."

I see a clearing in the woods; tree-stump stools border a burnt-out campfire. I know what this is, as hotel guests aren't the only people allowed here: An article on their website trumpets "Forest Adventures" ...

"Forest Adventures for children aged 5-11 ... shelter building, campfire starting and cooking, den building, and woodland exploration ... (And there's a photo of young children in delicious woodland — no path in shot — gleefully hugging a thick tree.) ... Being in nature makes most children very happy, the 2022 Children's People and Nature Survey reveals ... increases wellbeing and nature connectedness, developing a meaningful connection to and understanding of the natural world and our place within it ..."

The booking page says it costs £40 per child.

I bathe in Seeley Copse a while, then I walk around the parkland and Emperor's Brow — another forest treat for their hotel guests: "Dawn Chorus": "... an early morning outing to listen to a huge variety of birdsong ..." — and I come to The Kennels, their private members' club. I bumble around the car park for The Kennels, trying to find a way into a forest called The Valdoe — "PRIVATE" — but the woods are walled off, and I give up after thinking that I'm attracting too much attention being in a car park of Porsches and Lamborghinis but not getting into any of the cars; I look like a thief browsing ... So I take to the road — Kennel Hill — on the thin verge, again like a fox, to search for another way in, which I find by the "PRIVATE DRIVE" to Hound Lodge ... Hound Lodge, which was once home to the mutts used for the Charlton Hunt — the estate's infamous fox hunt that drew the elite of society, dukes and earls and lords. It's now a 10-bedroom luxury gaff that costs £10,000 a night to rent (plus VAT) — that price is insane but does include a butler and sauna and access to these "enchanting woodlands" (as described by their website) ... I enter the woods, a bonny forest that's huge, much larger than Seeley Copse, and I roam about for an hour, and I see no one.

From The Valdoe, I cross Pook Lane and come to a gate with a sign on it: "IC SS". Most of the sign has been torn off. I guess it originally said "NO PUBLIC ACCESS", but it could also have been "PUBLIC ACCESS", so I climb over the gate and walk along a lane that leads to the second golf course on the estate, the Downs Course. When I read in the Scottish Outdoor Access Code that Scotland allows plebs on golf courses, I thought: *What? Really?* So I dug into golf courses a little to see why that might be, and I read that less than half of any golf course is "cultivated" — fairway or green — so there's lots of spare space to walk. I also came across a heinous statistic: Golf courses in England take up hundreds of thousands of acres. That's not far off 1% of the country sealed off for damn golf — a "game" not even played unless the weather is agreeable, which in England it's often not. This golf course here has stately woodland and fine views of gently sloping, verdant countryside, and there are many paths that snake around and beside the fairways and greens. There are golfers here now, and lots see me, but none appear bothered about my stroll. And why should they care? Because I'm just walking around.

The reality of the right to roam is entirely different to what doom-struck gimps cook up in their weird minds. The reality isn't the improbable scenarios that worriers sketch in detail and then project to be the norm: "Someone will roam onto the Hole 14 green and take a fat dump!" The reality is simply people having a lovely time. Paranoid haters get very twisted, in particular, about the idea of people camping in their garden: "I don't want someone pitching a tent on top of my prized geraniums! We can't live in a society like that, a society where millions of people are roaming around camping on each other's flowerbeds!" They madly stress about that, which no one would do, yet never agonise about, say, people potentially parking on their drive now ... "I'll just park on that drive there instead of at a car park; save myself a fiver; why not?" ... That never happens; no one ever parks on a stranger's driveway, even though it would be easy to do. No sane person would do that. Just like no sane person would wander into a stranger's garden and camp in it. The right to drive obviously doesn't include the right to drive onto a stranger's driveway and park, and the right to roam clearly doesn't include the right to roam into a stranger's garden and camp — or the right to roam onto the Downs Course to defecate on the Hole 14 green. (Yes, I did camp on a golf course, which is the sort of scenario that Hyacinth Bartholomew from Puttenham panics about, but I only did that to make a point, and I wouldn't typically be a jackass like that. Camping on a golf course, camping in a "DEER RESERVE", camping in a "PRIVATE FISHING" place ... this is quite stupid, but I only camped in those spots as a fuck-you to the dukes, and to show you that their defences and security are weak. If I can camp in those stupid places, you can camp on the wider estate, away from the deer and golfers, far from the Big House, on the thousands of acres of meadows and woodlands.)

I leave the golf course up a steep hill, which brings me out in between The Trundle — an Iron Age hill fort — and Goodwood Racecourse: the track, the grandstands, the toilets, the bars ... Hundreds of acres of land off-limits so horses can be raced 19 days a year. I walk a path past the racecourse and through Car Park 4A ... Coach Park 7 is up there, and here's Car Park 8 — a sign says it's £15 to park there. Crisp packets and beer cans on the floor, crap from the 100,000 people that stomped through a couple of weeks ago; water bottles and coffee cups and packets of fags ... a blue catering wristband: "Qatar Goodwood Festival — Saturday 5th August 2023" ... This estate, on their website, talks of "stewardship" of the countryside, but, I wonder, how many thousands of trees were felled for this racecourse that's bounded by woodland? How many thousands chopped for all the car parks? And these grandstands that are a blight on what's otherwise succulent scenery, how's that "stewardship"? The neat parkland in front of the house, surely that was woodland before, and what about the motor circuit and the aerodrome and all that? The golf courses? And how about the land leased to Rolls-Royce that I yesterday walked past? I came to a roundabout on the estate, and off the roundabout led The Drive, where was gold lettering on a purple sign: "ROLLS-ROYCE". Since 2003, their manufacturing facility has been here — a stain equivalent to 24 football pitches. Apart from all that, they're "custodians" of the countryside ... It's such bollocks. The dukes claim to be "stewards", to be "custodians", to be "guardians", but what they are, what they really are, are "security", "sentinels", "bouncers" — bullying people off the land. They've converted the countryside into a private members' club, and you and I aren't invited.

Near the racecourse is Goodwood Country Park, the only free public space on the estate — for walking; a sign says: "NO OVERNIGHT CAMPING". On the OS map, the Goodwood Estate *takes up more space than the entirety of Chichester*, which looks bad, so Charles tossed the locals this bean so he can say, "We *do* give access." It's smaller than the racecourse, smaller than either of the golf courses, smaller than The Valdoe ... It's much smaller than it appears on the OS map due to spiked fencing that blocks off 75% of the forest marked on the map. On the fencing is a sign: "NO PUBLIC ACCESS". What the hell are they doing in there? Why do they need people kept out? It makes you wonder, right? It makes you suspicious ... Secretly snaring badgers? ... Sacrificing children? ... They'll say, I bet, "Sorry, really sorry, but it's not safe. We cut trees there, forestry operations, blah, blah, blah ..." But I saw at Huddleton Estate what forestry involves, I knew the foresters there, and forestry is, basically, planting some trees and felling some trees, and they're not doing the latter every day, and never after 17:00 or at the weekend. And, anyway, chainsaws are noisy as hell; if you hear a chainsaw, you avoid that area. You'd need the unlikely combination of a deaf walker and a blind forester for there to be any risk.

Out of Goodwood Country Park, I walk north through woodlands larger than The Valdoe, on the same footpath that runs alongside the racecourse. It's a public footpath; on this estate, it's one of almost none. This one that skims through the north of the estate is named the Monarch's

Way, and its history is linked to the great-great-great-great-great-great-great-great-great grandad of today's Duke of Richmond: Charles II ... The path roughly follows the route taken by Charles II during his escape after being trounced by Cromwell at the Battle of Worcester in 1651. Charles I had been executed two years earlier, and the fisticuffs at Worcester were Charles II's attempt at acquiring the throne that had been his dad's, but he failed and was forced to flee. There was a bounty on his head, and anyone caught helping him faced death. Charles, aged 21, adopted a peasant accent and disguised himself with ill-fitting, coarse clothes and a wonky haircut. He was on the road for six weeks, sleeping in woods, ducking behind hedges, hiding in barns, cat and mouse all the time — no doubt trespassing quite a lot, and maybe he even spent a night on a golf course. He, at last, reached the south coast, where he sailed for France and the protection of his cousin King Louis XIV. Charles spent the next nine years in exile, a time in which England was without a monarch and governed by a republican regime. Only after Cromwell succumbed to septicaemia did cowardly Charles return. He was on the throne by 1660 and siring kids with his many mistresses; the offspring were made dukes or earls, and we still have some of their ancestors lording it now: the Duke of Richmond, the Duke of Buccleuch, the Duke of Grafton ...

This path starts in Worcester and finishes at Shoreham, and with all its twists and turns, it clocks up 990 kilometres. I'm not, actually, averse to staying on a path; it's often simpler — less stingy and brambly, and less likely to get lost — but there just aren't enough paths. Like, this woodland I'm in right now, this giant forest, has only this one slim footpath through it, and the rest is gated and fenced off with barbed wire: "GOODWOOD ESTATE — PRIVATE — STRICTLY NO PUBLIC ACCESS" ... On the path, I come out of the woods onto a grassy slope that looks over East Dean, a pretty village ... The Star & Garter tavern, a blue tractor ploughing, cows in a far-off field, some sheep — *baaaaaaaa*. A lush quilt of greens and hearty woodland under a bright, blue sky. English countryside at its mighty prime ... From East Dean, still on the Monarch's Way, I cross a couple of fields and pass into woods named Red Copse: exquisite, timeless forest that it's easy to picture Charles II scuttling through on the lam, with his XXL smock and his terrible hairdo and his pretend bumpkin accent, a fugitive fleeing, not giving a flying damn about the law ... It's absolutely perfect for a blissful night in a little tent, but even here, miles from Goodwood House, Charles II's great-great-great-great-great-great-great-great grandson makes the rules; a sign next to the path says: "GOODWOOD ESTATE ... THIS IS PRIVATE PROPERTY & YOU'RE TRESPASSING ... LEAVE IMMEDIATELY ... YOU ARE ON CCTV".

Leave immediately ... Trespassing ... CCTV ... And the joke is: *I'm in a national park.* These woods are in the South Downs National Park, as were all the "PRIVATE" woods I've rambled through today ... and, so too, Goodwood Racecourse and the two golf courses ... I've been in the South Downs National Park since I yesterday climbed that fence into Car Park A. 92% of the Duke of Richmond's estate is within the South Downs National Park (says their 2022 Sustainability Report). He's not the only duke who owns a slice of it: the Duke of Norfolk does too. A bunch of viscounts and barons also own some of it ... There's a common misconception about our national parks: that they're owned by the government; they're not. In the US, they are, for the most part; the US government owns Yellowstone and Yosemite and others. But not here in England; here, the vast majority of our ten national parks are in the hands of private individuals, some of whom are dukes ... Over a quarter of Dartmoor National Park is owned by the Duchy of Cornwall, and a fat chunk of Northumberland National Park is part of the Duke of Northumberland's kingdom, and the Duke of Devonshire's massive estate is within the Peak District National Park ...

The Peak District National Park was the first in the country, and the only reason we got that was because people fought for it ... Kinder Scout — the highest point of the Peak District — is 30 km from Chatsworth House and also 30 km from Manchester, and the Duke of Devonshire didn't like the idea of grimy townies on a weekend escaping the industrial, toxic city air that foully choked them Monday to Friday, didn't want those grubby peasants walking on his land. He couldn't accept that, so the duke hired an army of goons to keep the plebs at bay. But one Sunday morning, the paupers fought back ... Led by a bloke called Benny Rothman, a Manc horde of hundreds heeded a rallying cry to "take action to open up the fine country at present denied to us", and they trooped to Kinder Scout in protest against being barred from the land. Rudely accosted by henchmen with batons, it got messy: bruising scuffles, arrests, jail. But it made the newspapers and the public sided with the plebs. In court, asked why he'd done it, Benny said, "After a hard week's work, in smoky towns and cities, we go out rambling for relaxation, for a breath of fresh air, for a little sunshine, but we find the finest rambling country is closed to us. We're denied the pleasure of enjoying, to the utmost, the countryside." He later wrote that the trespass was to stand up for "the rights of ordinary people to walk on land stolen from them in earlier times".

That was in 1932, and in 1951, after a lot more fighting, the Peak District became a national park. Now, national parks cover 9.3% of England, which, as a number on a page, looks ace — "Nearly 10% of England is national parks!" But that statistic means sod all, as our national parks are, in fact, mostly "PRIVATE".

TRUST ME, EDDIE

I'm laid in long grass atop Nore Hill, in the shadow of the Folly — a lone, fancy archway to nowhere; laid among crickets and butterflies and ladybirds and bumble bees, as I listen to a fantasy football podcast and wonder: *Should I transfer Watkins for Alvarez?* A couple of pensioners on a nearby bench, nattering, and a man and his son walk by, eyes pinned to whopper cameras. I gaze at the plush greens, the plump sheep — *baaaaaaaa* ... at the flat, low-lying stretch to the sparkly Solent ... I can see the Isle of Wight, I can see West Wittering — where Siobhan and I camped on the beach.

Last night, I camped nearby on a sheep farm. Not wild camped, but camped at a campsite a stone's throw from the Monarch's Way. I fancied a shower and needed a water refill; £15 a night. I was the only person on the campsite. Excellent, I thought, as I chilled and enjoyed the peace ... then eleven teenagers arrived. They drank, they smoked, they partied; they laughed and swore and sang. I couldn't sleep until 03:00. I'd have had words — "Lads, look, come on, give me a break. I sweatily slept on a golf course last night, and I've walked a half-marathon today, and I *need* to sleep." — but I knew it would end in a scrap, and II v I are bad odds. I'd then be turning up at the Duke of Norfolk's estate — where I'm wild camping tonight — looking an awful mess.

I'm not on Charles's Goodwood Estate now, but I'm not very far from it. This is the Slindon Estate, a neighbour of the Goodwood Estate; the two are so close that they just about touch. This 3,500-acre estate isn't owned by one of the dukes or viscounts or barons. It's owned by the National Trust. They own about 4% of the South Downs National Park. Across England, nearly 2% of the land is theirs, which is nowhere near the 25% hoarded by the aristocracy. The dukes, the barons, the marquesses ... those lot serve themselves, whereas the National Trust, in their words, "Are Europe's largest conservation charity, looking after nature, beauty, and history for everyone to enjoy."

This free-to-visit estate is stitched with rights of way that criss-cross around and about; not one, not two, like on dukes' estates, but dozens of paths, here and there and everywhere, thoroughly dissecting the land. It has 40 km of footpaths and bridleways, and I spent this morning meandering around a mellow tapestry of Englishness, along stony paths, winding tracks, and shady lanes ... up and down rolling green hills, past flint farm buildings and cottages, through pastures of hundreds of sheep — *baaaaaaaa* — and big fields of brown-and-white cows ... breeze whispered through flowering meadows that flared with yellows and oranges. In the tranquil landscape were pottering people: a gran with her red-head grandchild plucking berries, a hand-holding couple with a golden Labrador, birdwatchers with binoculars ...

Now, from the Folly, I walk into the forest behind: Nore

Wood. This is open access woodland, some of the 900 acres of open access woodland on this estate, woodland where you don't have to stay on a path. This is how forests should be, so you can immerse yourself in the woods, not be simply funnelled through like you're visiting some attraction. I roam freely in the cool, dark wood, its floor dappled and crunchy, go into the depths of the forest, dissolve myself within it, get high on nature: I touch trunks; my hands stroke the bark. I look at freaky fungi — shaggy parasols, earthballs, inkcaps — and I sniff flowers, see deer skipping merrily, listen to the birds ... and I think about what co-founder of the National Trust Octavia Hill said: "We all need quiet, we all need space, we all need beauty."

They do forestry sometimes in these woods, and, at one spot, I see stacked logs; I also see a National Trust sign that sets out where and when they're doing upcoming forestry work; it says, "Please respect notices closing parts of the woodland or any of our contractors requesting that you use an alternative route at that time. We apologise for any inconvenience." A very logical approach to forestry, as there is in Eartham Wood, which borders Nore Wood ... Yesterday, on the Monarch's Way, I walked through those sprawling, sublime woods, which are part of this estate but are on a 999-year lease to the Forestry Commission. That forest has lots of side paths and tracks, and it's without barbed wire, and no signs shriek "PRIVATE" or "KEEP OUT". The one sign I saw, when I entered the woods, said: "Forestry Commission ... Parts of this forest are temporarily closed to public access." Note the key words there: *parts* ... *temporarily*. It's a grand place to camp for a quiet, restful snooze in nature, is full of flat, soft, shady spots, far from any path ... But the Forestry Commission are anti-camping;

their website says "wild camping isn't permitted" on their land. Their stance is different to Forestry And Land Scotland, the government agency that looks after Scotland's forests, who say on their website: "We encourage responsible wild camping" — and, on the same page, say: "The forest is a magical place at any time of day. Why go home when you can stay?"

In the south of the estate is a quaint village: the blue and yellow of Ukraine flies, and outside a whitewashed cottage is a table of eggs and a hand-drawn notice: "Six Free-Range Eggs — £1.99 — Help Yourself. Leave The Money In The Box." The Jubilee Orchard is brimming with blackberries and big, red apples and juicy pears, and a sign there says, "Pick an apple, pear, or plum to supplement your lunch, or take a bowl of fruit to turn into a pie, tart, or crumble." A cafe sells steak-and-stilton pasties and Scotch eggs as large as cricket balls; on its "Dog Menu" are Linda's Cheesy Biscotti Dog Treats. The National Trust have an office in the village beside what was once the Big House — before the National Trust acquired the estate in 1948 — but is now a school. I'll go to the office to ask them about wild camping ... I know it's not allowed because on the back of a National Trust sign that I saw were small print by-laws: ... 4(b): No person shall throw a boomerang or use a lasso ... 10(b): No person shall waterski ... 13: No person shall pitch or erect a tent, booth, windbreak, clothesline, shed ... 22: No person shall use indecent or obscene language ... But I suspect that though the official policy is that they don't allow wild camping, the real policy, the one used day-to-day on an estate like this, is that they don't mind, is that they're unofficially aligned with the National Trust For Scotland, who say on their website: "Nothing compares with a night of wild camping and getting close to nature in a remote, beautiful location."

A guy is in the office, sitting on a big, black chair, tapping on a keyboard. I ask, "What's the policy of the National Trust for wild camping on their estates?"

He says, "I know for sure you can't camp at East Head, which is a National Trust spot on the coast near here, a Site of Special Scientific Interest."

"Right, sure, but that's a Site of Special Scientific Interest; what about everywhere else, all the places that aren't Sites of Special Scientific Interest?"

"I'm not sure. I'll Google it." He taps away a little, then says, "I'm still not sure. But you'd be better off going to a designated campsite, I think."

"You must get wild campers on this estate? What do you do with them? Kick them out?"

"I've never seen it, actually, never seen any wild campers here."

"The estate's pretty big. Maybe people camp here, and you just don't know about it? It must be hard to know what's going on across so much land?"

"Yeah, it's difficult. We can't have a ranger walking around, driving around, all day and all night, keeping an eye on everything. We can do that at East Head, which is much smaller than here; there, on weekends in the summer, because it's particularly popular there, a lot of tourists, we have a ranger there all the time, to look out for fires and parties, but we can't do that here."

And that's a good reason to welcome people and give them wide-ranging access: the visitors here are extra eyes to look for deeds that shouldn't be being done ... If I see some tosser with a disposable barbecue, I'll deal with that; if I see a yobbo chuck a Pepsi bottle in a bush, I'll sort it; if a pervert has his winkle in a sow, I'll slap him ... Visiting eyes are also on the "custodians", though, which is perhaps why the dukes are keen to keep us away, so nature boffins can't give them a hard time: "That doesn't seem right, all that gunk you're spewing in that river ... And those Chinese chemicals you're spraying on that field, is that legal? ..."

This estate's snowflake of footpaths, its open access woodland, is a model that Duchyland could use. Why not? If the National Trust can do it on this estate, this estate that's sandwiched between the Duke of Richmond's and the Duke of Norfolk's estates, why can't it be done across Duchyland? It could be done, it absolutely could, but the dukes are like spoilt toddlers refusing to share: "MINE!!! This is mine, mine, mine! No share, no, not want share, NO, NOOOOOOO!!! MINE!!!" Which is the vibe as soon as I leave the village and cross a field and a road to enter the massive estate of the Duke of Norfolk — or Eddie, as he's known to friends. The first forest here, Madehurst Wood, has a muddy, churned-up public footpath through it, and Eddie doesn't want us leaving the footpath, doesn't want us to enjoy this forest: Signs nailed on trees bawl: "PRIVATE WOODS — KEEP OUT". Yes, well, whatever ... I roam off the path and through the woods, and there's no one around, no chainsaws nor machinery, no reason the public should be kept out.

I pass into Rewell Wood and through there to some fields where two red tractors are making hay as the sun shines, and I see poppies growing in the wild grass, and I gobble blackberries. In the distance are the turrets of a castle — Eddie's home. It's been Eddie's castle since 2002, when his father, the 17th Duke of Norfolk, passed away. His father inherited the dukedom in 1975 from his second cousin once removed, who died without having a son.

Second cousin once removed: that's a pretty tenuous connection; the DNA shared between a person and their second
cousin once removed is about 1.5%. How Eddie acquired
the dukedom is simpler: He was the eldest son. Not the
eldest *child* but the eldest *son*. He has three older sisters,
whom the dukedom passed over to be his. One of Eddie's
nieces — the daughter of Eddie's eldest sister — is pretty
pissed off about that. Her name is Kinvara, and she told
Town & Country magazine that primogeniture — the law
that sees these titles and estates pass to the eldest son —
was "absolutely mad". She said it was "bonkers" that we still
have these "antiquated rules". Kinvara's father is Roderick,
the 5th Earl of Balfour. He and Tessa — that's Eddie's
eldest sister — have four daughters but no son. That
means the title Earl of Balfour will pass to Roderick's
brother, not Roderick's children. Kinvara told *The Telegraph* that it's "ridiculous". She said "women are disregarded entirely" and that "women's rights to fair treatment
are being violated". She said: "With these titles comes the
chance to be elected to one of the 92 seats still reserved for
hereditary peers in the House of Lords, which have been
held almost exclusively by men." She fumed that her eldest
sister, Willa, will "not get a seat in the Lords to help make
decisions about our nation. What a pity." She called on the
Prime Minister to "end this injustice, bring the aristocracy
into the 21st century, and give the daughters of hereditary
peers a fair chance to take up seats in parliament."

She has a point, no doubt, but her wording is a little off;
here's my edit: "Peasant's rights to fair treatment are being
violated. It's ridiculous! Because of these antiquated,
bonkers rules, paupers are disregarded entirely. With these
titles comes the chance to be elected to one of the 92 seats
in the House of Lords still reserved exclusively for the aris-

tocracy. That's absolutely mad! No pleb can get a seat in the Lords to help make decisions about our nation. What a pity. We must end this injustice, bring down the aristocracy, and give plebs a fair chance to take up seats in parliament."

I enter Screens Wood and see a sign stuck on a gate that's topped by barbed wire: "NO PUBLIC RIGHT OF WAY". The sign doesn't state that it's Eddie's land. He's quite discreet about it, not using his name or coat of arms; he instead makes all his signs the same colour: blood red. I follow a path that takes me past some cottages — their doors and eaves and window frames painted blood red — and I walk through woodland, see more barbed wire, more blood red signs telling me where I can't go. This is a public footpath, and it's overgrown and brambly, and I get stung by nettles and scratched, and it abruptly dumps me on the A284, next to Eddie's Arundel Park. I can't access Arundel Park because around it is a three-metre-high wall ... I mean, I can't access it *here*; there's a footpath through the middle of the 1,200-acre park, but to get to that path, I have to walk along the A284 for twenty minutes; walk twenty minutes along this busy road, this busy road that has no path next to it. So I'm again on a narrow, grassy verge, a man turned into a hedgehog, dangerously scampering along the highway, cars whizzing inches past me.

Eddie couldn't drive down this road for a while — or any other road ... Last year, he was banned from driving for six months after being busted in London for speeding through a red light while chatting on his mobile. He already had nine penalty points on his driving licence from previous speeding offences. The Duke of Rutland — David Manners — is a naughty driver too: In 2016, he was caught speeding four times in eight months — once going

75 mph in a 50 mph zone — and was thus banned from driving for a year. And, in 2021, David's daughter was nabbed speeding in Brentford on the M4 that slices through Boston Manor Park. She was fined only £50 after she ticked the "yes" box on the form that asked if payment of the penalty would cause "financial hardship". Charles, the Duke of Richmond, was a teenage joyrider; he told *The Sunday Times*, "One day, when my parents were out, a friend and I borrowed a Land Rover and tore around the fields. We were doing well until my friend accelerated through a gate and stuffed it straight in the side of a bloody horse box. It was totally annihilated." He said another time, when he was 16, he drove his mother's Morris 1100 into a tree. When old enough to legally drive, he said in an interview with the magazine *Luxury London* that he once hared his Porsche 924 Carrera GT from Goodwood House to Chelsea in just under an hour; that's a 60-mile journey, and if not breaking the speed limit, it would take at least 90 minutes. He also said that on the day the 70 mph national speed limit came in — that was in 1965 — his grandfather, the 9th Duke of Richmond, *protested* by driving flat out up Edgware Road in London. (He was nicked for that and ended up at Bow Street Magistrates' Court.)

That right there is stone-cold proof that *some* dukes drive like dicks ... thus, *all* dukes — in fact, let's say *all* the damn aristocracy, *all* the earls and barons and viscounts and marquesses, and, now I think about it, *all* bloody coun- tryfolk — *all* of them should all be banned from driving in cities ... "You can't be trusted to bring your car to an urban place because you're from the boonies. We have multi-lane roads in cities, and we have signs you've never seen, and zebra crossings and mammoth roundabouts. You'll park in the wrong places. You'll drive too fast, or you'll drive too slow. You'll crash, cause an accident: People will die. So KEEP OUT!" No, that would be foolish, obviously — as foolish as arguing that townies can't be trusted to wander around the countryside without leaving a path.

The A284 takes me into the town of Arundel, where blood red is rife on gates and doors and window frames and drainpipes. I see Cockburn's Tea Rooms, the Norfolk Arms Hotel, an antiques store with muskets and Chinese porcelain figurines in its window. I see a war memorial: " ... Alfred Carver ... Victor Wilson ... Herbert Stewart ... Reginald Prangle ... Ernest Page ... Those who, at the call of King and Country, left all that was dear to them, endured hardness, faced danger ... giving up their own lives so that others might live in freedom." A plaque near the war memorial says, "Since William rose and Harold fell, there have been Earls at Arundel." That William, of course, is William the Conquerer; as for the Earl of Arundel, Eddie's that too, as well as the Duke of Norfolk. His full name is Eddie Fitzalan-*Howard*, and he's part of one of the oldest aristocratic families in Britain, who have their paws all over the ~~free~~ land that Victor, Alfred, Ernest, Herbert, and Reginald died for ... The Earl of Suffolk is Alexander *Howard*, a descendant of the 2nd son of the 4th Duke of Norfolk; he has 4,500 acres in Wiltshire. George *Howard* is the Earl of Carlisle, and he's a descendant of the 3rd son of the 4th Duke of Norfolk, and he has 2,000 acres in Cumbria. Castle *Howard* is a 9,000-acre estate in Yorkshire, and Greystoke Castle and its 6,000 acres near the Lake District have been *Howard*-owned for centuries ... Eddie's kingdom isn't only his acres around Arundel; he also has estates in Norfolk and Yorkshire, and altogether has over 40,000 acres — more than 22,000 football pitches.

Eddie kept me out of his park for a while earlier, but he

won't be keeping me out of it tonight ... I enter through a
large gate by Park Lodge, and I see a sign: "NO CAMPING".
The sign says it's illegal to wild camp here ... Is it, though?
No, it's not. And, anyway, this "park" is the size of 680 football pitches — 30% larger than the space where Glastonbury is hosted. This isn't a park but an estate within an
estate, and it's too large for them to know what's going on
... In 1989, the lake here, Swanbourne, dried out and
revealed a WWII German bomber plane that no one knew
about. If a plane survived unnoticed for forty years, I'm
sure a tiny green tent will slip under the radar for a night.

I head north through the parkland on a path, through
long grass, up and down gentle hills, beside swathes of
fenced-off woodland ... I see sheep — *baaaaaaaa* — and I
see adverts: the same advert for the same company, again
and again: Fauna Brewing ... That's one of Eddie's businesses, which I know because, as a member of the House
of Lords, he has to declare his "interests": He's a "person
with significant control" at Fauna — a beer brand inspired
by wildlife, with each beer named after an endangered
species. He's President of Arundel & Littlehampton
District Scouts, and he's a trustee for Houghton Estates
and Cholmondeley Estates; these are ~~tax dodges~~ trusts for
the Marquess of Cholmondeley. The Houghton Estate in
Norfolk is 4,000 acres, and the Cholmondeley Estate in
Cheshire is 7,500 acres.

I break off the path and walk beside Dry Lodge Plantation, where I see some pheasants, and I see a shotgun
cartridge on the ground; the woodland, a massive space, is
ringed by triple-stacked barbed wire ... I jump a padlocked
wooden gate at the brow of a hill, and I'm at Duke's Plantation. With high-powered binoculars, Eddie could see me
here from high up in his castle, and he might be on the

lookout for me as I did email him. (He didn't reply.) But is
Eddie in his castle? He's just as likely to be in London, drag
racing the Duke of Richmond along the Strand ... Those
speeding aristocracy stories I highlighted, note the location of most of them: London. The dukes are very, very
keen on denying the plebs the cream of the countryside,
while they have the best of both worlds: Peregrine
Cavendish's children weren't born in a barn on his estate;
and David Manners doesn't carve his wife's Crimbo
presents from oak trees felled on his 16,000 acres; and
when Andrew Russell runs out of Fist It lube, he isn't
restocking at Woburn Village Store ... The dukes need
London, Milton Keynes, Sheffield, Chichester ... They go to
those places, them and their crew — their butlers and
woodsmen and farmers and grunts — they go to cities and
towns and gorge on the best of urban living, then they
retreat to their rural estates and whine about us wanting to
feast on the finest countryside.

And this spot here, beside Duke's Plantation, this is
very, very fine, and I stand for a long while to dine on the
view: the soft, sloping greens, the chunky, majestic forests,
the proud, grand castle, the English Channel — which
William boated across with his army 957 years ago, landing
on these shores not far from where I stand. His army was
small: 7,000 or so. That was all it took to conquer a country
of 2 million people, which was the population of England
in 1066. We're at 57 million these days; a lot more people
squeezed onto land that hasn't gotten larger. Many prime
slices of that land, like this spot here, are off the paths
we're ordered to stick to. But we don't have to stick to those
paths. The land we live in today was unjustly divvied up
centuries ago, but we're now in 2023, a time when dukes
and barons and earls can't shatter your skull with a

crossbow for refusing to bend the knee. They can tell us to keep off their land, tell us to stay on the paths, but can they make us? No. So don't keep off their land, don't stay on their paths; roam free, see what you find ... You may find a spot like this, a spot ideal to see a regal sunset blanket a castle in night, a quiet space of beauty to repose under the stars in a tiny green tent and ease into a serene, meditative, higher state to await a gentle whisper of wisdom on whether to transfer Watkins for Alvarez.

THE BOSS

A towering granite wall; on the other side is the town's gloomy, Victorian-era Big House. I walk beside the burly wall to an arched, guarded gateway; a sign says: "WELCOME TO HM PRISON DARTMOOR". The Acid Bath Murderer stayed here, as did The Mad Axeman. Now, it's sex offenders, mainly. Across the road from that dark, stark, sinister ugliness, its barred windows and razor wire, is the prison museum in what was once the prison dairy. Crude garden ornaments outside, painted garishly: bunnies in dresses, hedgehogs on see-saws ... made by the rapists and nonces at the prison. "FOR SALE": Prices start at £6. Inside, I speak with a spectacled, chubby Welsh man at the front desk. I say, "The prison is owned by the Duchy of Cornwall, right?"

"It is, yes."

"And the Prison Service lease it from them? Do you know what the deal is with that? I went to the Duchy office earlier, but no one was there, and I'm sure they wouldn't anyway tell me."

"You're talking to the right man: I know all about that.

Until a year ago, £1.3 million of taxpayers' money was going into Charlie's pocket for that old, damp dump, every single year. But the lease was due to end this year, and instead of renewing it as they'd always done, someone at the Prison Service wised up and realised they were getting ripped off, so the Prison Service said they didn't want it any more. That was a problem for the Duchy, as they'd be lumbered with a huge white elephant. You see, it's a Grade II-listed building, and it can't be altered, even for making security improvements. It can't be turned into some sort of odd hotel or something. Knowing that, and knowing there are 670-odd prisoners in there, and those would need to be rehoused somewhere in a prison system already stuffed, and knowing it would be terrible publicity — the Prison Service saying Dartmoor was closing because they were being fleeced on the rent — knowing all that, the Duchy said, Actually, maybe you can have it for free; yes, sign this long-term lease so we don't have to deal with that shitty building that's falling apart; sign this lease so you have to deal with that, and instead of paying £1.3 million a year, as you have been, you can have it for £0. And the great thing now is that the £1.3 million that was being paid to Charlie can instead be invested in the prison: repairs, security, education programs, staffing, things like that."

This prison wasn't mentioned in *Inside The Duchy Of Cornwall*, a documentary I watched last week. It was filmed in 2019, on the 50th anniversary of Charles being the Duke of Cornwall ... The documentary started at a garden party at Restormel Castle — part of the Duchy's portfolio — where Charles was giving a speech to scrubbed-up farmers: "Ladies and gentlemen, for me, the great joy is to see so many of you here whose fathers were tenants when I first became involved 50 years ago ..." He ended with a quip:

"Thank you, ladies and gentlemen, for paying your rent every now and then. I've tried to do useful things with it."

The narrator said, "Farming may be the face of the Duchy, but today, the lion's share of the estate's £21 million annual profits comes from big-city investments and commercial property."

It cut to William walking through the countryside at Englishcombe in Somerset, one of the Duchy's largest estates. "It's a cracking spot," said William. "Lovely views," said one of the four plump, suited blokes with him — senior Duchy staff — and with an expansive sweep of his hand, the bloke added, "Duchy to the horizon." William then met the Keeling family, who have been farmers there since 1938. "This farm has been my life. I was born here," said Mervyn Keeling, who was due to pass it on to his son. As they looked at some cows, William chatted to Mervyn about the countryside, about the importance of children being in nature, and the narrator said that William was, at that point, living on the 20,000-acre Sandringham Estate. Over tea and cake, there was talk of Brexit and the end of EU farming subsidies, and William told Mervyn that he'd chatted with sheep farmers who were worried about surviving financially. They might be less worried, I thought, if they didn't have to stump up rent each month to the Duchy — rent for land acquired by the Duchy for nowt.

The narrator said: "The duke takes personal pride in the woodland at Llwynywermod, his Welsh home ..." That's a 192-acre estate, owned by the Duchy of Cornwall, just outside the Brecon Beacons National Park, that was bought in 2007 so Charles could have a Welsh retreat. Charles was shown there, talking about trees, and then he was at his 350-acre estate at Highgrove; he was there with a flat-capped bloke, Roger, who had shaggy mutton chops: "I'm the Chief Steward of the National Hedgelaying Society ..." Charles is patron of that society, so Roger said lots of nice things about him; as Mervyn did earlier. Though, of course, no one would slag off their landlord/patron when being filmed for a documentary about their landlord/patron.

Charles talked of "sustainable urbanism", then the scene shifted to Nansledan, a development started in 2013 on 540 acres of Duchy land. The Narrator said, "Eventually, 10,000 people will live here in 4,000 homes. But with just 300 built, the challenge is clear." Charles said, "It's going to take, what, 40 years, I suppose, to be completely finished." Charles said he goes "down and around, twice a year" and was then shown turning up there in a flash car. Duchy staff lined up in a car park to meet "The Boss" — as they referred to him. Then Charles went on a "whistle-stop tour" of Nansledan. 30% of it is "affordable housing", they're proud to boast. But flipping that statistic means 70% *isn't* "affordable housing".

Next, there was a little party on the roof terrace of 10 Buckingham Gate, the Duchy headquarters in London. Pol Roger champagne was sipped. The Chief Executive of the Duchy of Cornwall was there: Alastair Martin, a man paid £318,000 a year. Some Duchy farmers were there too; Alastair said he wanted to "give them a bit of a treat". Five Duchy tenants received this treat; two of them were Mary and Justin Adams, who'd come to London for the day from their farm in Somerset. Justin said, "My family have been Duchy tenants since the mid-1800s."

Charles was then shown in Cornwall, which he said he tries to visit once a year: "We just stay for a couple of nights," he said. While there, he stayed in a 500-year-old

Duchy manor house, which the narrator said is available to the public to rent for £10,000 for a week. Charles zoomed by helicopter from there to Truro to visit a new tenant on a 200-acre plot of Duchy land. The new tenant was Rhys, who'd sold his house in Wales and ploughed all the money into buying 30 Aberdeen Angus cows. Rhys said, "I suppose it's the same as any other landlord coming to see a new tenant."

The show ended with Charles at Balmoral, the 50,000-acre royal estate in Aberdeenshire, within the Cairngorms National Park. He was ambling around the luscious grounds, reminiscing about 50 years as being The Boss of the Duchy of Cornwall. He was asked: "What does that make you feel when you see your son talking to Mervyn, talking about succession?" Charles said he was "deeply touched". It then cut to William telling Mervyn, "I've started to think about how I'll inherit the Duchy one day and what I'll do with it."

Now William has inherited the Duchy, inherited its 130,000 acres, its profits of £24 million a year — up £3 million since 2019 — and one thing he should do with it is sort out crappy Princetown ... The prison is in Princetown, and the whole town is awful; it feels like I'm in Bulgaria. There's no doubt it's Duchy-owned as the "PRINCE-TOWN" black sign on the way in is stamped with the Duchy emblem: the inverted triangle of yellow spots that I saw fly over 10 Buckingham Gate. It's full of tired, stained terraces with rusted satellite dishes, and tatty, ashen houses with paltry front yards full of junk and trash. On the anorexic high street is a convenience store with scanty shelves of obscure brands, a cafe serving fry-ups and fish and chips, a charity shop. Its library is open seven *hours* a week, and the one bus in and out runs three times a day.

It's very, very different to Nansledan and Poundbury (another Duchy "community", near Dorchester in Dorset); the Duchy always brags about those two, and their website displays photos of both: neat streets, colourful houses, happy faces. There are no photos of shabby, depressed Princetown.

William visited nearby Wistman's Wood this July, which I know because there are lots of photos of him in a flat cap and swish cashmere sweater — knitted in Bergamo, retails for £295 — looking pensive as he talked about "sustainable stewardship". That ancient woodland is 9 acres, less space than the prison takes up. He came for a PR photo — "Look at me! I love trees!" — but doesn't appear to have dropped by tumbledown Princetown to visit the poor tenants paying the rent that lets him buy Luca Faloni jumpers. Because Princetown isn't on-brand for the Duchy, like their B&Q store in Milton Keynes. They don't want a photo of William knocking the door of No.24 Burrator Avenue to ask for his rent money — "Pay up, damn pleb!" The Duchy of Cornwall want to appear as farmers, as "stewards", not as a £1 billion empire headed by a landlord that pockets £65,000 every day. Because of their branding, I'm sure some people mistake it for a charity. And, to be fair, the Duchy of Cornwall does make donations, as highlighted in their 2023 annual report: "In the Benevolent Fund's last financial year, it made grants and commitments of £261,000 to a variety of charities." It says, additionally, that, "Charitable donations made by the Duchy of Cornwall estate amounted to £109,000." So, yes, they do donate to charity; they donate 0.015% of their profits.

The Duchy office — their regional headquarters — is next to the Duchy Hotel, one of the town's oldest buildings. I go to the office again and knock the door, but again, no one answers. The hotel is no longer a hotel; it now houses the National Park Visitor Centre. It houses it *for now*, but not for much longer ...

> *Mid-Devon Advertiser*, 2nd Feb 2023: "**Six-Month Reprieve For Dartmoor National Park Visitor Centre At Princetown:** ... The centre was due to close early this year to save Dartmoor National Park Authority (DNPA) money as it faces a shortfall of £500,000 due to reduced government funding ... The DNPA has postponed the closure until the end of September while extra funding is sought to keep it open ..."

I wonder: Is the cash-strapped Dartmoor National Park Authority handing over taxpayer money to William for this place? I ask the woman inside, and she says the building is leased from the Duchy, but she's unsure if the lease is a freebie or if they're paying for it. I guess they're paying for it, as if the Duchy were happy to pocket over a million a year of taxpayer money from the Prison Service, they're happy to gouge anyone. Because raking in rent from as many people as possible is how they get a profit of £24 million a year, not from growing organic carrots. Princetown Primary School? Yeah, probably paying the Duchy rent, as is the library that's open seven hours a week. And the Ministry of Defence? Very likely, I'd say; very likely paying millions to the Duchy so that the army can train in north Dartmoor — which they do: live-firing exercises up there, mortars and tanks, over 100 days a year shooting up and shelling one of our ten national parks. The Duchy might not be invoicing the Dartmoor National Park Authority and Princetown Primary School and the

Ministry of Defence, but other than little tidbits, no one knows what they're up to, no one knows where the profit comes from or what it's spent on. An MP who led an inquiry into the Duchy of Cornwall in 2013 said, "There's little transparency." It's beyond my amateur sleuthing, and Sherlock himself would likely fail.

When the Duchy Hotel was still a hotel, Arthur Conan Doyle visited, and it was here, in 1901, that he wrote *The Hound of the Baskervilles*. That story about an aristocrat being menaced by "a foul thing, a great, black beast", was set in Dartmoor, a place Conan Doyle called "so vast, and so barren, and so mysterious". That was one of 62 Sherlock Holmes stories that Conan Doyle wrote, all of which have been in the public domain since 2000, 70 years after Conan Doyle died. Because that's how copyright works in the UK: it expires on the 70th anniversary of the author's death. I, today, could plagiarise his descriptions of Dartmoor, and it would be fine. You, today, could write a whole story about Sherlock Holmes and publish it without asking for permission from anyone, and the profits would be yours. If a Sherlock Holmes movie comes out now, Conan Doyle's ancestors receive zilch. It's the same with music: 70 years after the artist's death, the copyright expires. If my great-great-great-great-great-great-great-great-great grandson records a version of *Shape Of You*, Ed Sheeran's great-great-great-great-great-great-great-great-great grandson won't receive a penny from the sales. And neither should he because he did nothing for it; he shouldn't leech off long-dead Ed. And yet the dukes, their estates ... it's forever; now and always. The Duchy of Cornwall — as I said early on this book, this book that will be in the public domain 70 years after I die — their land has been with them since 1337. That's 686 years.

A Jail Ale at the Plume of Feathers while I read *Inside Time* — "The National Newspaper For Prisoners" — then, as a low-flying Chinook thunders overhead, I walk into wide-open space, rugged vastness, and soon all trace of tragic Princetown is behind, and I'm upon the bosom of the brutal moor, a great, devilish wilderness. Slate clouds crawl over its low, long, sombre curves that are dotted with strange monoliths and topped by jagged granite crowns. Here and there on boulder-strewn slopes are stunted, twisted trees, bent out of shape by the ungodly temper of storm after storm. It's not quite a storm now, but the wind howls and a steady drizzle slowly soaks me, and I'm glad I opted for the riding boots ... I was again in Birmingham looking a fool, this time stood on New Street's Platform 10B attracting baffled stares, but better that than headlining tomorrow's *Devon County Chronicle* ...

"**Dipstick Rescued From Dartmoor:** Dartmoor Search & Rescue yesterday saved the life of a man from Birmingham who thought it would be okay to hike across Dartmoor in flip-flops. At 11:50, less than an hour after he'd set out, he dialled 999 and said, 'I've made a terrible mistake'. A helicopter was deployed, and he was spotted near Vixen Tor, muddy and barefoot after losing his flip-flops in a bog. When asked why he wore flip-flops, he said: 'I thought the OS map was exaggerating about the mires; you know, artistic licence.' Psychiatric testing is being conducted to establish what's wrong with the man. Peter Swaine, who led the rescue, said, 'He smelled delightful, which I know because he insisted that I sniff him, but he's clearly mentally unstable. I mean, what sort of an idiot comes to Dartmoor wearing flip-flops?!'"

A few miles from Princetown, I take cover under a contorted, skinny tree, beside the crumbled remnants of an abandoned tinworks, to wait for the rain to ease. This was the lair of the great, black beast, the spectral hound that Holmes duelled with, and before me is the Grimpen Mire of the book ...

"A false step yonder means death to man or beast. Only yesterday, I saw one of the moor ponies wander into it. He never came out. I saw his head for quite a long time craning out of the bog-hole, but it sucked him down at last."

Its real name is Fox Tor Mire, and I'll cross it, which isn't as crazy as it seems as the OS map shows a route through it, a green line from this side to the other ... After the rain has eased, I set off into the miry marsh, and all is going perfectly for a short while; the ground is a little spongy, sometimes quivering like a poked jelly, but I've faith in the map ... Then I recheck my phone, as I've been doing every thirty seconds, and the map shows me well off the green line. *How the hell did that happen?!* Right, well ... I'll just walk back to the green line, and that's fine until ... FUCK!!! It's like a tenacious, malign hand has hold of my foot and is tugging me into the miasmic depths of a filthy, dark pit. I haul my leg out and look about, trying to work out my exact steps that got me into this mess so that I can retrace them out of it. I inch along uncertainly, braced for a false step that will suck me into the bowels of Dartmoor, and I manage to trace my way back to the old tin mine. There I bump into Alan, Adrian, and Gareth, who are kitted out in cagoules and waterproof trousers — not skinny jeans, like me. I tell them the pickle I got in, and Adrian says, "One got me once. I was in up to my chest."

"Your *chest?!*"

"Yeah. These guys had to pull me out. I was covered in slime and shite, soaked through. I'd still be there if it weren't for these two, as I literally couldn't move. I was stuck."

"Where was that? Dartmoor?"

"Yeah, Dartmoor. There are bogs all over this place."

They're bound in the direction I aborted, so I join up with them and return to the oozing morass. We get to near the point I reached before, and they pull out their compass and paper map, but it's no more use than my app was. We rock-paper-scissors to see who will head the line — it's Gareth, with me second — and then on we go, jerky, zigzag progress through the slushy, insidious quagmire, sticking to grassy tussocks where possible, precariously stepping with jittery care, non-stop cursing the whole time.

We, at last, reach firmer ground, where I part way with them, and I'm again alone on the wet, wild moor, still on Duchy land, as I have been since leaving Princetown, and, for hours, I stumble slowly along lumpy, sodden, squelchy ground, through browny, coarse grass full of big slugs, slog up then down, up then down, on and on and on, the rain beating upon me, the wind whistling about my ears. It's hard going, and it's clear why that prison was built here: stick the worst of the worst in the middle of bleak, harsh terrain, a remote, treacherous landscape littered with stinky bogs. This is land where we don't have to stick to a path, one of the few places in England where that's the case, but this land is offal, is odious compared to the succulent sirloin of the South Downs, and I think: Surely William can offer us more than *this* to roam freely around?

He has a lot of acres that are far, far nicer than *this* ...
William owns most of the Isles of Scilly, a place of "out-
standing natural beauty"; and his Guy's Estate is 11,000
acres of "peaceful and beautiful surroundings in the Here-
fordshire countryside". He has land in Kent, Wiltshire,
Shropshire ... and I bet that land is better than *this*. The
Duchy's holiday cottage website lists properties in all sorts
of places that are sweeter than this gnarly void: Henver
Cottage lies within "beautiful Duchy countryside in the
north of Cornwall"; a three-night stay in September is
priced at £1,067. Trendeal Barn on their Arrallas Estate —
"... a wealth of countryside and woodland trails ..." — is
£2,096 for three nights. And Dairy House (£2,502 for a long
weekend) is at Restormel: the Duchy's "historic estate of
rural beauty".

But we can't walk free on any of that land, can't camp
on any of that land; no, not legally; instead, William offers
us *this* — dour, desolate, melancholic moorland.

He *could* declare, "Peasants, as a man of the people, I
say that all the land of the Duchy of Cornwall is open to
you, my dear paupers, open to you to roam and enjoy! So
go to my land, go there to walk and to swim, go to my land
to fly kites and camp and be free!"

He *could* do that if he wanted because he's The Boss.

A noisy stream, gushing swiftly, is the border between
William's estate and the estate of his neighbour ... His
neighbour Dickwart. I wade through the stream, then toil
up a steep slope to a lonely summit, a steep slope of long,
brown, squidgy grass, a dire, muddy trudge, and I crest the
summit wishing for a fine vista of green and lovely
England ... But no: more dreary contours of dismal moor;
more long, brown, squidgy grass; more mud. I'd camp here
if I could, as I've had enough, walked far enough — seven

hours — but this ground is absolutely rotten, is too lousy for camping: too soggy, too bumpy, too exposed. Of everywhere I've visited this year, this is the worst land by far — the land I've crossed from Princetown to reach here. If I'd known *this* was what I was protesting for in January, I wouldn't have bothered; I'd have stayed in bed on that grey, frosty morning.

It improves slightly, after a while, as I near the edge of the moor, near the place where Old Crockern was conjured, where that merry pagan troupe of elvish women skipped and clapped and hollered: "... Wooooooo yah! ... Hey-a-hey-ahhhh ... Yeeeeah! ... Ye-ee-ee-oooooo ..." I see, two miles away, the village of Cornwood, and, far off, see Constable-like landscape, that fine, green England I've seen much of this year, that glorious England which has given much joy. And I see, right in front of me, Bronze Age abodes on this scarred hillside, stubborn stone huts in which slumbered neolithic, hairy men. The roofs are long gone, but one will do fine to pitch my tent in, with what's left of the walls giving some protection against the lashing wind. And they don't just have walls; they also have doorsteps, which is exactly what I need to yank off my boots.

I pitch the tent as a thickening shadow is veiling the moor, and a swirl of eerie, white vapour is brewing, and I'm just in time as soon comes savage, appalling weather, a hellish storm that makes me wish I wasn't under the stars but in a comfy Travelodge. The rain pours terribly, and there's vicious thunder, menacing lightning, and so severe is the wind that I fear I'll lose my tent to the vast gloom. As I lay awake, tossing restlessly — ... 01:00 ... 02:00 ... 03:00 ... — the haunting darkness breeds noises: neolithic footsteps, galloping horses ... and the wicked, fierce wind carries with it a long, low moan, sweeping over the moor, carries agonised sobbing that swells into throbbing, roaring anger that sinks into muffled sorrow, a murmur of strangled distress ...

It's not a foul thing, not spectral, ghastly evil, I tell myself to sedate my fright. No, it's Dickwart suffering loudly, still not over the news that Vos, Newey, and Underhill unanimously overturned the High Court ruling from January. It's poor Dickwart in despair, pained and crying, not able to accept that he can do nothing about piggy peasants roaming across his land with tents to spend a night on the moor.

NOW WHAT?

Wild camping allowed on 0.2% of England is absurd, as is 8% of the countryside available for walking, especially when Duchyland alone is 25% of *our* great country. The dukes and barons and marquesses and viscounts and earls won't open that 25% for us, but so what? We can open it for ourselves if we want; we can go there, get on with it, live free.

I say *we*, but I mean *you*, as I need to vanish after lobbing a bookful of barbed stones at awfully wealthy, probably litigious, people. I have that law degree from a top-114-ranked university, so maybe they won't want to mess with me, but it's very hard to sue a man who they can't find, who bolted the country on a one-way ticket to ...

THE END

It starts in El Ceibo and ends in the Amazon; a savage journey in between, by bus and boat through Americas central and south. Along the way, a failed revolution, a spewing volcano, a drawer of cocaine; and a surreal assortment of oddballs and freaks.

www.gonzo.schule/amerzonia

EL CEIBO TO GUATEMALA CITY

A man the size of two men, biceps as thick as my neck. He's at a desk, on a chair large enough to be a throne, staring at me squirm on the sofa. My butt is sticky with sweat from the faux leather. His henchman, who forced me to come to this dingy room, is stood beside him, doubling the sullen eyes on the prey. Door closed. Blinds drawn.

"Pay," he says, his expression emotionless, the perfect poker face.

I say, "I'm not paying."

The more I protest, the less English he speaks, the more bullying his attitude. He soon speaks only Spanish.

I glance at the door: I could make a run for it. But the

door may be locked, and I don't know where I can run to. I'm in the middle of nowhere, on the border between Mexico and Guatemala. And on the other side of the door are men with guns.

The room grows smaller with each second, slowly crushing my defiance. But I have some left: "I'm not paying," I say again.

He scowls, says, "*No pagas, no te vas.*" Don't pay, don't leave. Said with an absoluteness that permits no argument.

Gatekeeper is used as a metaphor; he's a literal one, in charge of this gate out of Mexico. He won't let me leave until I've paid £20 for a tourist permit. But I paid when I entered the country. He knows I've paid: it's impossible to enter Mexico without paying. Under the pretence of officialdom, I'm being mugged. He knows I know there's nothing I can do about it. He's the judge, the jury. If I continue to refuse, he'll tell me to sod off. It took me four hours to get here. To get to another border crossing, I'll have to return to Palenque and travel four-plus hours south from there — where I may have the same issue. Or he'll plant drugs on me. Not a sizeable amount — it wouldn't be believable for me to traffic against the north-bound tsunami — but a gram or two he could get away with.

"Can I pay by card?" I ask.

"No."

"Can I get a receipt?"

"No."

I pay. I've no choice.

I call him a twunt as I'm leaving, wrapping it up with a Merry Christmas — "*Feliz Navidad*, you twunt." — to avoid suspicion. It's a safe insult, I think — surely he won't know that? Then I panic that he'll Google it, so I quick-walk off

— as fast as I can go without running — past pickup trucks with cargoes of people, past swindlers primed to sting: "*Señor! Señor!*"

I got here — the border at El Ceibo — via a through-the-night journey from Mexico City. Before boarding, airport-style security: IDs checked and bodies frisked, luggage scanned and searched. The driver locked in his cabin, the glass tinted and bulletproof — shielded from bandits and the stink of chow mein, which several passengers brought on board on paper plates from a cafe at one stop. I had a seat next to the bog; if we were ambushed, I could have used it as a panic room. I'd have taken my chances, however, because the toilet was vile, the toxic whiff like a soiled diaper on a warm day. Drop-down screens with volume dialled to granny-friendly prevented sleeping. Now, a battered minivan speeding along a narrow, hole-studded highway to Flores in the north of Guatemala. No one wears a seatbelt because there are none. Trucks hurtle at us, thunder close by; the road barely wide enough to squeeze in a couple of passing vehicles. Some cross their chests, whisper prayers. They're right to do so: beside the road are burnt-out chassis, victims of long-ago crashes. Names of the dead are spelt in stones on the canvases of hillsides.

The station at Flores is a frenetic jigsaw, its many pieces in motion. Dust rises from wheels and footfall; people cover their face, cough and splutter. Some spit, some piss on walls. Shoeshiners struggle for silk purses from pigs' ears; the shinees on wooden thrones, paupers playing princes. A guard with a shotgun outside a shop — one selling day-to-day items, not diamonds. Pilfer a pack of Oreos: BANG. You're dead. I've no such protection. It's a sad state of affairs when you're worth less than a pack of

Oreos. Cries of "*Agua, agua. Fruta, fruta.*" Others stick their head in minivans to peddle socks and batteries, medicines and fireworks. Someone's selling a framed picture of a woman posing sexily on all fours, a waterfall photo-shopped in the background.

I board a minivan bound for Sayaxche, south of here on my screenshot of a map of Guatemala. The distance on the map isn't far, but the terrain between there and here is unknown. How long it will take, I've no idea: an hour or seven or twelve. I don't mind. Days like these on the road are some of the best on a trip like this; thinking and observing, channel-surfing, catching glimpses, flashes, bits. I'll ride until darkness draws down a veil, then bed down until sunrise. Where I don't know; I'll deal later with detail. No need to stress: always a town of some sort or size, always a hotel, a store. I won't sleep on the streets. I won't starve.

The van is buggered. One window cracked like a snowflake, stuck with sellotape. Strapped to the roof are soiled suitcases; also bicycles and sacks of all sorts, tied tenuously in place. My bag is on my lap. Any bigger and it would need to go on top, exposed to thieves, to the elements. It's the litmus test for those who say they travel light: if you're not comfortable with your bag on your lap for hours, it's not light. I have only 7 kg in my bag. I'm without all but the essentials — and also without several essentials: no towel, no trainers, no smartphone. (An iPod Touch is my only tech.) I have flip-flops and boots. A wise man packs hiking boots. A wise man I'm not: I've packed Chelsea boots.

Seats soon full. Plastic stools put in the aisle — soon full too. Several stand. One with a chicken; a live one, its feet and beak tied. Quetzales go out through windows;

plates of tacos come in. Others buy fried slices of bananas or strawberries coated in chocolate. Crumbs tumble from mouths, adding to those already on the seats and floor. I'd pity the person who had to clean this van if such a person existed. We cruise about town with the door open, scouting for extras. Somehow squeezed in, another four children and three chickens. A butt nudges my face; a baby sucks a breast, close enough for me to suck the other. A girl sings Christmas-sounding songs. I'd prefer a Christmas-sounding silence. All but me are locals. My blue eyes give away that I'm not of this parish, that I'm a wanderer wandering, but no one's bothered about my presence.

I'm taking a locals' *colectivo* — rather than a tourist shuttle — to hide in plain sight. Desperadoes, I reason, are less likely to hijack a minivan of paupers than a busload of foreigners. Still, to be on the safe side, I have money stashed all over: various pockets and parts of my bag — even down my sock. A thief might empty my pockets and take my bag, but steal my socks, surely not. Paranoid? Maybe. But with reason: Guatemala is ranked as one of the twenty-five most dangerous countries in the world. It's fifth for gun-related deaths per 100,000 people. Police are overwhelmed: A force of 30,000 for a population of seventeen million. 90% of homicides remain unsolved. The past scars the present: endemic violence a legacy of the civil war that ravaged Guatemala from 1960 to 1996. Torturing, kidnapping, murdering. The police, the military, the government as guilty as anyone. At the end of the war, an amnesty was granted for even the worst crimes. No one was accountable.

As bad as it is in Guatemala, it's far worse in Honduras — twice the murder rate of Guatemala. And El Salvador — three times. I'll have to pass through one of those on my route south to the Amazon, where I'll go balls deep into the depths of the jungle to drink ayahuasca, a sacred tribal brew. William S. Burroughs — the original ayahuasca tourist in the 1950s — said it was the strongest substance he'd ever experienced. "It is like nothing else," he said. "This is not the chemical lift of C, the sexless, horribly sane stasis of junk, the vegetable nightmare of peyote, or the humorous silliness of weed ... This is insane overwhelming rape of the senses ... It is space-time travel ... You make migrations, incredible journeys ..."

Should I be in Guatemala? Should I be journeying overland to the Amazon through savage states so I can take the most powerful hallucinogenic known to man?

Yes. Dare to roll the dice, I say; risk a one for a six. And it's a story to tell. Life should be about stories. "So, anyway, this one time a narco shot me ..." What a shame, what a waste, to be sat in the old farts' home and have little to reminisce, be short on tales to tell.

"Grandpa," says Little Johnny, "tell me about your life."

"I worked in an office for fifty years. At weekends, I went shopping, I watched TV, I drank beer."

"Is that it?"

"Err, let me think ... oh, and I married your nan ... and nine years later, we divorced."

"Anything else?"

"No, that's all, basically."

"Oh," says Little Johnny, frowning. "Will my life be like that?"

"Your life, Little Johnny, will be different. You can be anything, do anything. If you want, you can be a pirate. A princess, if you prefer."

Then they hit eleven, start at big-boy school, and the bubble is popped. Dreams of being an astronaut are no longer tolerated. "Be an accountant, Little Johnny; that's where the money is, that's what pays the mortgage."

And so it starts: A lifetime of slaving and saving for a life that never gets lived.

Plus, it's worthwhile to disappear now and then, to go AWOL from reality for months: in your absence, friends and family remember only your finest qualities; they forget your faults, forgive your wrongs. It's almost as if you've died. On your return, the red carpet is rolled, and you're treated like the resurrection. But you have to disappear for at least half a year to places considered dangerous. A month in the Maldives won't do.

Out of Flores, a tropical landscape unblemished, as green and wild as Mother intended. The largest settlements barely stretch back from the road they straddle. Hardly a building is higher than a storey. Huts for homes, shacks for shops. Walls of wood; roofs of steel, of thatch. Some are concrete, bland and grey as the day they were built. Homes to be lived in, not looked at. To the residents, these communities are coloured and intricate, but what can I see in a passing second but that which is obvious, and what is obvious is poverty. It's more like India than Mexico. Mexico is more like the US than here. Breadline living, basic as can be, is the norm for Guatemalans: 55% live in poverty; 29% in extreme poverty, on less than £2 a day.

The road dead-ends at the bend of a river, the Rio de la Pasion. "Coban?" I ask the driver, the next town on the map.

He points over the river.

A motor canoe ferries me across. On the other side is Sayaxche, a town of dusty roads, of bumpkin commotion and bumbling disorder. Vans come and go; none set for

Coban — their destination known via a sign in the windscreen or the shout of the driver. There's no ticket booth, no timetables. Purgatorial waiting ensues. It could be an hour, could be three. I may end up sleeping in Sayaxche. This is travel: A series of faltering transitions. Uncertainty is what you sign up for.

After a time, a driver breaks from yelling a destination that begins with R to ask me where I'm going.

"Coban," I tell him.

He doesn't understand.

I tell him again.

He still doesn't understand but tells me to get in the van.

I get in.

Coban doesn't begin with R, but I don't have to go to Coban. What is it to me but a strange name on a map? On this journey of long-distance aimlessness, wherever I am is where I'm meant to be. Each place is as worthy as any other. So on I go, on the move towards an uncertain destination, a destination that's only a destination until it's reached; then it becomes a departure.

After two hours, the van stops at a crossroads. The driver tells me to get out.

"Here?" I ask, gesturing at nothing. We're not in a town, not even a village.

"*Si,*" he says, and more I don't comprehend.

I get out, hope the part I didn't understand was that vans to Coban, or to somewhere, will drive by, pick me up.

A van does soon come, from the direction the previous one sped off to. It stops for me. "Coban?" I ask.

He nods.

It's packed beyond capacity, of course, but I jump on board anyway, not wanting to chance getting stuck at this spot. This van also has a cracked window: the windscreen, the whole width of it. The interior panels are missing; the sliding door, at times, slides itself open. The only thing in good shape are the speakers — blasting eighties synth-pop. The driver's in a rush — they all are. He tries to overtake a truck on a bend, failing to see another oncoming at full throttle. Catastrophe narrowly avoided. He does the same again at the next bend.

This leg is on a remote stretch of road through Alta Verapaz, the greenest and wettest region in Guatemala, where on steep slopes sprout coffee and cardamon; through villages of indigenous communities where livestock wanders loose: flower-patterned blouses, flowing pleated skirts; babies stashed in slings on backs. Some sat like sages, stories written in their wrinkles; others at shacks, selling fruit. There a fellow riverside, panning for silver, perhaps gold. There one leading a donkey laden with firewood up a sinuous footpath to a lonesome building: a smoking chimney, holed linen strung on a line. The road rises and falls as it sweeps on through a densely-forested mountainscape — summits masked by mist. The rain just falls, the fierce downpour turning crater-sized potholes into swimming pools, and obscuring the driver's view; as does the steaming of the windows. With the rain, the steam, the crack, and the many stickers of Christ, he can see almost nothing.

Coban is drab, of no note; and Salama, the next stop, nondescript if you're generous, dreadful if you're not. A place to come to go, and the next place to go is the capital: Guatemala City. A bus this time, not a minivan; a so-called "chicken bus" to be precise: a decades-old school bus, a hand-me-down from Big Bro up north. At the end of their shelf life in the States, they're sent south for a new lease of life as a wackily-painted deathtrap. Besides a coat of paint, this one's jazzed with cuddly toys and a sound system that could hold its own in Ibiza. An eclectic playlist: sugary ballads to pulsing techno. Why bus drivers insist on playing dance-floor bangers, I don't know. No one on a bus wants to dance. What they spent on the sound system, they should have spent on the suspension: my organs are rearranged. These buses weren't designed to be driven at such speed. Haste to race ahead of other buses — to be first to pick up passengers — and also to thwart attacks: Gangs MS-13 and Barrio 18 govern here. To curb the gangs, there are police pickup trucks with swivel-mounted weaponry patrol; I saw them in Mexico, and I see them here: those aboard wearing combat gear, their faces masked with balaclavas.

The sun has set by the time I reach Guatemala City. A murder rate fifty times that of London. And even that is understated: The police don't count it as a homicide if a victim leaves the crime scene alive but later dies from the injuries. I want to hop on a bus to Antigua, 45 km away, but this is the northern bus terminal, and all the buses here go only north — where I've just come from. I ask at the information counter about hotels near the station. They say there are none, that I need to get a bus to the city centre. I board the bus they tell me to, the *Transurbano*; the others on board are mainly blokes, expressions chiselled to fuck-you. Outside, a teeming dystopia: Scummy suburbs sprawl, and on slopes are tacked dimly-lit shantytowns. Septic streets of chain-link fences and graffitied shutters, of scattered garbage and strewn liquor bottles. Heads pop up and peer, then quickly disappear, like urban whack-a-mole. Sinister weasels scuttle between cinder block boxes, skulk in the shadows. The discarded destitute fester: Rows of tents, ripped and stained, for block after bleak block; also dens and tarps and lean-tos, soiled mattresses and filthy, threadbare furniture.

Half an hour passes with me staring through the mucked window at signs that don't speak to me, thinking I can't get off here, or here, or here. I'm still hoping for a Starbucks or McDonald's — something that signals it's a safer spot than others — when the bus stops and everyone gets off. It's the last stop. No choice but to walk, but to where? Asking randoms where to go will show my hand, out me as lost and alone to them and anyone around. Fine in a rural town in the day, not in a homicide hotspot at night. So I stand on a corner and look up the four streets, assess which has the most life, and walk down that one. I do the same again, and again, and again, follow the flow of people, follow it past beat-up buildings and glowering doorways and gutters choked with trash, past shops that have their fronts barred like cells, past scraggy mutts and scrawny children in scruffed clothes, their glassy eyes focused on the faraway. Hustlers and hawkers accost, alcoholics stagger and slur. Some curled up on flattened cardboard boxes beneath boarded-up windows; some wrapped head-to-toe in blankets, looking like body bags. The vibe is gnarly, and I'm a beacon. The stares speak, but there are words too: "Faggot," someone shouts. Twice I'm asked for money; one moves his hand down the back of his jeans; a knife, an itch, I don't wait to find out: I run.

I see a hotel — Hotel Reforma — as shite as a hotel can be; I head for it. In the foyer is a waterless fountain; a Christmas tree, somehow wilted even though it's plastic. The room is a film set for a suicide. A lightbulb blinks sallow light on a grimed bedsheet, a 2009 calendar hangs. Television bolted down; toilet roll holder padlocked.

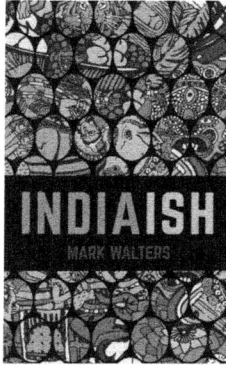

INDIAISH
MARK WALTERS

Mark rides buses and trains across Himalayan mountains and Rajasthani deserts, to super-cities like Delhi and Mumbai, and sacred spots like Varanasi and Rishikesh. He sees bodies barbecued beside the Ganges, goes insane when he drinks bhang lassi, visits the cult of "The Mother" ...

www.gonzo.schule/indiaish

RISHIKESH

Within the shitcake I've been eating, Rishikesh is a sweet, glazed cherry. Nestled in the forested foothills of the Himalayas, the Ganges bisects the town, and flows fresh from the mountains, free of faeces and corpses. On its banks, bells ring and chants float from ancient, colourful temples; ensconced within are *sadhus* and pilgrims, praying and prostrating, searching for salvation.

It's famed for being the cradle of yoga. Now hippie types flock to the town, the faithful and the freaks shopping in India's spiritualism supermarket. They join the locals meditating and contorting beside the sacred river.

The guys try very, very hard; to impress the ladies, I suspect, because there are no bars or clubs in this town. Being able to perform a flawless Macarena under the influence of a dozen Jagerbombs holds no sway here. Unless a guy can touch his toes — without bending his knees — and talk about *kundalini* for fifteen minutes, he has no chance of getting laid.

Around town, every shop and cafe has included a New Age word in their name — Freedom or Babylon or Krishna. Pinned to noticeboards inside are headshots of people purporting to be masters but who are patently muppets. The services advertised are manifold: reiki healing, tarot readings, trilotherapy sessions, consciousness maps, spiritual awakening — to name only a few. The one offering, "A journey into the time tunnel through soul molecule activation to appear in different time-space realities of human history," isn't a joke.

I had thought to spend a week in one of Rishikesh's many ashrams, places where you live a monk-like existence and spend all day doing yoga and meditating and sweeping floors. They're part fat camp — for people who have piled on mental rather than physical weight — and part cult, where you bare your spiritual hole for a bearded bloke to poke. It turns out, however, that International Yoga Week is next week, and so all the ashrams are booked up with people perfecting their postures and poses. But I'll still get my yogic groove on via some drop-in classes.

I've never tried yoga, but I may be a yoga person who just doesn't yet know it. I like tofu, I like whales, I like sitting down — the signs are there. I decided I'd need yoga pants and went to a shop earlier for that purpose, but when there I couldn't go through with buying some. I tried a few on, looked in the mirror, and thought I looked ridicu-

bend that way or that far. It's not my fault — it's genetics: my Dad has had both knees and hips replaced. I'm built from shoddy materials.

Swami eventually concedes that I'm as much a lost cause as a eunuch attempting the Kama Sutra. He starts giving me separate instructions to everyone else: "Everyone do x, y, z. Except you," and he points at me. "You just stand there and put your hands on your head."

Next comes pairwork exercises, and I get paired with Thierry. We lock limbs and push and pull each other; the result is something between a UFC match and recreations of erotic Italian sculptures. Thierry is, of course, better at the exercises than me. I'm complicating what would otherwise be easy for him. We're like Siamese twins, where one is in good shape but has an extra head and random limbs awkwardly attached.

When Swami tells us to take a rest, I assume it's the halfway point. I lay there looking like Stephen Hawking, wishing I'd prepared a contingency plan for this, as a debacle was always on the cards considering I haven't even jogged since 2014. If only I'd forged a note from my Mum saying I need to leave early for a doctors appointment. Shiva shows mercy on me, though: it's the end of the class.

It would be wrong of me to say yoga is a sham, nothing more than a ploy to shift excess stock of clown pants after the demise of circuses. I tried my best, but it wasn't a fair test on the merits of the practice. The test needs to be redone by someone more flexible than a plank of wood.

After a few hours interlude, I return to the scene of my yoga crime for something which should be simple: a class on meditation and mindfulness. Swami arrives ten minutes late; he says he forgot there was a class at this time. I don't know how much confidence I can have in a mindfulness teacher forgetting about his own class on mindfulness.

No one else has come for the class, so I'm one-on-one with him. After we sit, he starts with a warning: "You must know that meditating can bring up feelings of misery, despair, loneliness."

I think: That might explain the one-man attendance.

He says we'll work through some techniques he developed during a several-month stint in a cave in the snowy Himalayas. He has me huffing and puffing, moving my chin up and down, and adopting peculiar positions with my arms.

For the last technique, he tells me to lay on my back with bent knees and make a noise that sounds like "shoe" on every inhale and a "ha" noise on every exhale: "Shoe haaaaaaa, shoe haaaaaaa, shoe haaaaaaa ..." He leaves the room while I do this, and I lay there alone for fifteen minutes keeping it up: "Shoe haaaaaaa, shoe haaaaaaa, shoe haaaaaaa ..."

When he comes back — by which time I can "shoe haaaaaaa" like a pro — he tells me to stop and lay there quietly with my eyes closed. As I lay there, I feel a warmth that starts in my toes rise slowly up through my body. I think: This malarky actually works: I'm a believer!

Then he says it's the end of the class and to open my eyes, and I open them to see he's put a portable heater by my feet.

In the evening, I attend a talk by a guru — Shri Prashant — at the Tree House Ganga Cafe. Three times today, I've been given flyers for the talk. The flyers declare Shri Prashant the founder of the Advait Movement and make a couple of bold claims: "The purpose of Advait is for the creation of a new humanity through intelligent spirituality." And: "His unique spiritual literature is on a par with the highest words that mankind has ever known."

The room the talk is held in is made from bamboo and wicker. Shri Prashant sits at the front on a cushion throne. He wears a yellow scarf and tracksuit bottoms and woolly socks. His appearance and demeanour are that of a baddie in *Scooby-Doo*; one who plots for world domination but is scuppered by meddling kids and their dumb dog. He's very precise about how the room is set up: no one can sit on a chair and no one can sit next to anyone they know — and he also says all phones have to be handed in and that we can't leave until the end. One guy walks out on hearing he can't have a chair. Everyone else — about thirty of us — sits on mats in a compact semi-circle around Shri Prashant.

He has half a dozen assistants. They were the ones handing out flyers earlier, and now they scurry about as per his commands. He gets them to give out double-sided A4 sheets printed with Bible teachings. He asks us to read the handouts, and then he sets about roasting Jesus, picking holes in the teachings. "Don't focus on the prophets of the past," he says. "Those like Jesus come and go. You need to be open to new prophets and know that they may have a different appearance to previous ones. Open your eyes; you're missing what's in front of you."

What he says over the next hour is wishy-washy; spiritual-sounding but lacking structure and specifics. If someone questions his nonsense, he closes them down and tells them they don't understand, that they're "scared of the truth". But many in the room have glazed expressions and hang off his every word. Some make notes — me too. I worry Shri Prashant will see me writing and ask me to share my thoughts. I don't want to read aloud that I've written I think he looks like a villain from *Scooby-Doo*.

Ninety minutes in — and by now a few have walked out — Shri Prashant goes nuclear: "I'm not going to sugar coat it. The people closest to you are those who will prevent your progress along the path. Do not stay attached to the false family of mother or father, brother or sister, husband or wife. They lead you astray from the truth. Leave them all behind for a new dynamic family. It is the only way for your salvation."

He eases off a bit after this with some random tangents, including five minutes on how squirrels live and what we can learn from their squirrelly ways. I mostly agree with his thoughts on squirrels.

I want to stick around to the end of the talk to catch the final hard sell and maybe get a free keyring, but my brain cracks three hours in after a twenty-minute back-and-forth about using the word "gain" in a spiritual context. I spring to my feet and make a dash for it.

Having Shri Prashant as my only Facebook friend would put a stop to endless baby photos in my feed, but I can't justify ditching everyone I know for a bloke that I share some common ground with regarding squirrels.

He's not the only one in town with a messiah complex. I've seen many wannabe messiahs here — both Indians and foreigners — walking around barefooted with feral hair flowing over their baggy tunics. They must be kept apart; friction is inevitable when they meet ...

"I'm the messiah."

"No, *I'm* the messiah. *You're* just a long-haired chump who can't afford shoes."

"Your mum's a long-haired chump who can't afford shoes."

"I have no mum. I was sent to earth by Brahma."

"Then who's that woman with the same surname as you who's the only one that follows you on Twitter?"

"Screw you, Dave."

"I'm not Dave; I'm Davarius."

"Your name's Dave, and you're a dickhead."

Fisticuffs follow; some scratching, a bit of hair pulling. Then they part; one to yoga class, the other to the time tunnel.

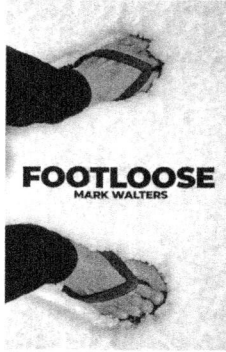

FOOTLOOSE
MARK WALTERS

Backpacking overland across Asia, Mark takes buses and trains and boats from Australia to Azerbaijan. He catches a cargo ship across the Indian Ocean, risks a dicey gauntlet of terrorists and Chinese tanks, has beers with a naked ex-Soviet officer in Kazakhstan ...

www.gonzo.schule/footloose

INDIAN OCEAN

Fremantle is a 25-minute train ride from Perth. At the entrance to its North Quay Harbour, a queue of trucks wait. I walk past them, past the eyes of the drivers looking down at the odd fella in flip-flops. I sit in the security gatehouse, waiting for them to check my story — my story of riding a freighter to Singapore. I get the all-clear, and a security guard drives me to one of the ships, drives me past giant cranes, past thousands of containers, past men in yellow jackets buzzing around. I climb steep metal stairs onto the deck, from where a Filipino bloke — Bernardo — takes me to a seven-floor structure towards the back of the ship that spans almost its width; in it are offices, bedrooms, dining rooms. My room is one of a few kept spare for journeys that require extra crew. It has a lounge, bedroom, and bathroom, and is furnished like a suite at a 3-star hotel. A TV, a DVD player, and a HiFi system (with tape deck). And towels: *Three! Decadence!* Everything is strapped in place, including an artificial potted plant in the corner — the straps to stop things falling in rough seas. Other signs that life at sea might not be smooth: A yellow hard hat and life jacket hang on wall hooks, and on a table is a large black holdall, a white label stitched onto it: "Solas smart suit type 2a. An insulated immersion suit / anti-exposure suit. Made in Scunthorpe."

Bernardo gives me an information booklet, tells me to wait in my room, then leaves. The booklet looks like it was created in the mid-nineties when clip art was cutting edge and anyone with Microsoft Publisher was a graphic designer. Images used include bananas, dancers, flowers — none have any relevance to the text. I learn that the ship is called MSC Uganda (but is German, not Ugandan). It's 294 metres long; it can hold 4,545 shipping containers. Those stats make it sound like a beast, yet it's one of the smallest ships here.

I wait, watch the cranes, snooze for a while, and slowly hours pass. The TV won't pick up a signal, and there's no wifi — the only internet access is via a computer in the captain's office. I'd like a walk, see what's what on the ship, but Bernardo said to stay put, and I don't want to piss off the crew at least until we've set sail and it's too late for them to kick me off. Noon passes, and still I wait. So much of travel is waiting, watching the clock: tick-tock, tick-tock, tick-tock …

After six hours idle in my room, I get a call on the in-room phone and am told to go to an office to meet the

that covers shipping my body back, as it can cost up to £10,000. I ignored that and got cheap travel insurance (because it was cheap).

Back to my room to free my feet in flip-flops, then I head up to the "bridge" — the ship's cockpit. In it is a steering wheel thingy (not the official nautical name), a large control panel with hundreds of buttons and dials, and three monitors — two display radars and one a map. The map is super detailed; it shows not only where land is but sea depths and danger points. I see that we've detoured around an area marked "Explosives Dumping Ground". Bernardo is currently controlling the ship. He says he does two four-hour shifts here a day. If it's daytime, it's a one-man job, but they have two up here at night as there's a risk that a man alone may nod off. It's a risk because there's not all that much to do. He tells me: "It runs on autopilot except when near land or when passing through a congested shipping lane."

"Punch in the coordinates, then chill?"

He laughs. "Not exactly. We still need to watch out for other ships. And keep an eye on the speed — reduce it if there are large waves to prevent containers falling off or damage to the ship."

"How often does that happen? Containers falling off?"

"It's rare, but it does happen. At my previous company, we lost three tiers during a severe storm."

I leave Bernardo to go down for lunch in the officers' mess-room, where I eat all my meals. A waiter serves us food; he calls everyone "sir" — he calls me it too. He looks a bit shabby, with DIY turn-ups on his black trousers (each stitch large and white), but still, always good to be a "sir". Proper food, a full-time chef — a nice change from Australia, where for two months I survived on tins of beans and canned fruit, bags of nuts and Kit-Kats. Spaghetti today. Yesterday, we had Chicken curry; another day, mashed potato and chicken steak; beef and boiled potatoes, that we had too, as well as chilli con carne. We sit at four tables of four, with everyone in the same seat for each meal. Sit in near silence; barely a sound other than cutlery, hardly a murmur. They must run out of things to say after months of sitting next to each other for three meals a day — especially when they have no news or weekends to discuss. There are only so many times you can debate the best size and colour of shipping container before the topic gets dull.

"Herr Ernst, did you see the game last night?"

"No, Ulrich, I didn't. We're on a ship; there's no TV. I never see the game. You never see the game. No one on this ship ever sees the game."

"Ah, right, of course. So what did you do last night?"

"Nothing. I was with you. We both did nothing. We sat and talked about how we did nothing the night before. We had this same exact conversation — like we do every night."

"That's not true; not *every* night. There was that one night we were so bored that we—"

"We must never ever talk of that night. Never."

Later, land ahoy! We pass palmy coasts, tropical islands covered in jungle. Asia: to be precise, Indonesia. To the left, the island of Sumatra; to the right, Java. This the Sunda Strait that links the Indian Ocean to the Java Sea. And here the sea is calm, and its colour changed: from a dark blue to a soft blue-green.

I watch the scene from F-Deck (the top floor of the ship), sat on a deckchair, the sun on my face, the wind in my hair, and think: This is a moment, the sort of moment to travel for. I think too that probably these are the best days of my life, the days of this trip — days past, days to come. I know that now and don't need longing hindsight. Here, now: The dream being lived.

"I'm jealous," some say. "I wish I could do that." And I tell them they can. Then they say, "I will, but next year, or the year after. Before I'm forty, 100%. Fifty at the latest." But I know they won't.

Others say, "Mark, shouldn't you settle down? Get married? A house?" I hear that more and more since I turned thirty a year ago. Asked by boring bastards, that settling-down question often is; those chained to their town, their norm, to a career, getting a mortgage; those bouncing between an office and a sofa, saving, boozing, and shagging, stockpiling cushions and shoes. The "done thing" done, day after day. Shitty drudgery, fussing at the margins, suspended in a vegetative stupor; counting the empty hours down to 5 pm, to casual Fridays, to a weekend of prosecco and Netflix. Quietly stagnating while simultaneously frantically posting Facebook photos to prove the opposite.

I've opted out of that life, opted into this one — a life that's uncertain, but a life that's chosen, not just the done-thing-default. As soon as real-life came, as soon as I sensed that suffocating routine, I set off for a more breathable atmosphere. I went to Thailand, went to Korea, went beyond. I swam away from the mainstream, and I'm still at it — doggy-paddling my way to ... well, let's see where. Maybe I can't do this forever — on the seas, on open roads, without obligations nor responsibilities, no compromises nor constraints — but I can do it for now, press the pause button for reality until I'm forty at least. The way I see it, most people live until they're about eighty, and those years should be split between being settled and being unsettled. Eighty divided by two equals forty years of each. So it mathematically makes sense not to settle until you're forty. You can't argue with maths. To think you'll work hard when you're young, then go wild when you're retired, is bollocks. By the time people retire, they're mostly worn out; their vigour and enthusiasm wilted at best, died at worst.

Now I have my youth, my health, and diamonds they both are. I won't waste them on a hunt for riches and respectability — that's for sure. Freedom: that's what those diamonds will be spent on. Freedom to go here, to go there, to go anywhere; to wake up when I want to wake up, to eat a bowl of Coco-Pops at three in the afternoon; to quench my fancies, to explore the cracks of the world, to seek for the weird and wonderful, for novelty and for awe. Oh yes — sweet, glorious freedom.

And so on this bench, this bench on the MSC Uganda, the MSC Uganda cruising to Singapore, I'm glad I've left all that — the prison of routine, the humdrum ordinariness — left it for days clothed in uncertainty, to go mining for the extraordinary, digging deep; one day finding treasure, the next a dead body or a turd. And I will have my reward, so long as all I want are laughs and stories to tell.

Back to F-Deck at 6 pm for a barbecue. Most of the crew are here; the Kiribatians as well, but they keep to themselves, don't mix with the Germans. We eat steaks and sausages, baked potatoes, garlic bread, salad, beans. And drink beers, lots of beers — bought from the ship's shop, which opens for an hour a day. The shop sells beers (£9 for a crate of twenty-four Warsteiner bottles) and cigarettes (£7 for a 200-carton), as well as Ritter Sport chocolate and other foodstuffs from Germany — little tastes of home to see them through the long months away.

As we eat and drink, I ask the captain what he does with his free time on the ship.

He says, "I have no free time. I get email after email to deal with. It didn't use to be like this. Ten years ago, I'd get one lot of papers when I left a port, and that would be it until the next port when I'd get more. Now, because of these auto-pilot ships, they think I should deal with the stuff they used to do in their offices. When I was a child, my dream was to be a captain, but I never dreamed it would be like this: doing admin all day long. I don't want to work like this, but what can I do? It's the way the job is now. Not like when I started, when to be a captain you really had to know how to sail a ship, and you'd be at the bridge all day, sailing — *really* sailing. These days, the younger ones don't know much, don't know how to sail. If you took their tools away, they wouldn't know what to do. But they're good with computers, with spreadsheets, and that's what the shipping companies look for now. And they also want yes-men, guys who do what they're told. The reason for the delay at Fremantle was that I wanted more fuel before we departed, but head office said we had enough. There was only 250 tons of fuel put by for us, even though I told them a month ago that we need 350. I told them that to leave without 350 isn't safe. We argued, and, at last, they gave in, and I got the 100 extra. Who made that decision to say we need only 250 tons? Someone in an office who's never sailed these ships. Whereas I've sailed for decades, yet I still have to argue about stuff like that."

A week I've been on the ship. We may reach Singapore today, but I don't know. There are only so many times you can ask, "Are we nearly there yet?" — and I feel I've already exceeded that limit.

I've by now stopped looking out my windows: there's nothing to see but sea. The seven DVDs here I've watched: *The Matrix*, *The Matrix Reloaded*, *Enemy At The Gates*, and a few others. One day, I went to the gym, pool, and sauna. Once was enough. The sauna is the size of a fat man's coffin; the pool is a small metal box filled with seawater; the gym has only three pieces of antiquated weight-lifting equipment. To properly exercise, the only option is to run in circles — small circles because there's no space to run in large ones. The crew go months at a time without any decent exercise, which (along with the stodgy food) explains the chunky bellies. They get paid well and aren't stressed or overworked — just eight hours a day they do — but the boredom must take its toll. Every day the same, just ticking them off until they can go home. It's a cooped-up existence and one I'd struggle with. For me, to be on board is a novelty, but a week is plenty to play at being a sailor. I'll be glad to be back on terra firma, where I can run in circles as large as I like.

At 1.30 am, an alarm sounds, then the phone in my room rings: the captain says a Singaporean immigration officer is on board and wants to see me. The officer stamps me into the country without asking any questions — like: "Why the heck are you arriving on a cargo ship?!" A local aboard selling sim cards to the crew says he'll drive me into the city for £18. *Do I like the look of this man?* No. *Would I leave him alone with my sister?* No. *Is he the only way for me to get out of here?* Yes. So I'll give him a go.

Soon after, I'm sat in a van with him — Tony Lee, he

says his name is — weaving through Singapore's streets. There's nothing to fear when arriving late at night at a place unknown with no hotel booked. Most will know the word "hotel" even if they know little to no other English. As for guidebooks, they're for beginners; they're travel-by-numbers, a comfort blanket. And are out of date as well: even if it's the newest edition — *Updated for 2014!* — there's a two-year lag from researching to publishing, and a lot changes in a couple of years. The best places — hotels, restaurants, whatever — for today are those that will be in tomorrow's guidebooks. To find them, word of mouth is everything, suggestions from travellers, from locals — from Tony Lee.

It doesn't always work out, this wishful rolling of the dice. You hope for the best but also must brace yourself for the appalling — and appalling is what the Hawaii Hostel is, the place that Tony Lee drops me, a place that seemingly survives on those too weary to be fussy. The receptionist is asleep across the check-in desk. After I wake him, he takes me to an ill-lit rathole without windows. Stains on the walls, scuffs and smears. £25 it costs, but I take it. For one night, I can sleep anywhere. I lay on the sagging mattress and think: I've done it; I've made it to Asia.

mark@gonzo.schule

www.gonzo.schule

Printed in Great Britain
by Amazon